# DEDICATION

This book is dedicated to those who have loved, supported and had confidence in me when at times I had no confidence in myself! Derek and Lois Williams who nurtured and breathed life into my faith when it was nothing more than embers. Haydn Williams, a true pastor and shepherd of the sheep, who visited my home and who cared for my family. Karen Lowe and Deborah Chapman who opened up their hearts, lives and church when few others were willing to take the risk. You crazy Welsh women, you loved me in the hard times and trusted me in what was obviously a 'bumbling revival!' I'm eternally grateful for you both! Sarah Trinder, transitioned but never forgotten! You wild, loud and obnoxious spirit, you put your arms around me when the system wanted to shut me down, I will never forget you. Justin Abraham a guy who was willing to connect with a total maverick in order to see something new birthed in our nation. Joanne Gravell a beautiful woman and friend, a true radical who was willing to remain when others moved on. Jo your support and love encouraged me to keep going when everything within me wanted to give up. You have no idea how many times I relied upon you and looked to you for help! I owe you so much x.

John Crowder; an irritant to the religious system, a fellow journeyman, a friend who stuck closer than a brother! Thank you my friend for loving me, trusting in me, sharing your hotel rooms with me and putting in all the administrative effort (which I knew nothing about) over many years. You helped me to have more fun and to stop taking myself so seriously, what greater lesson could anyone learn? I love you and honour you my friend. Benjamin Dunn, the sweetest spirit on the planet, you not only *taught* me how to love but *showed* me how to love! Your commitment to the poor and your unwavering trust

in humanity challenged me deeply and shattered all of my apathetic frameworks regarding mankind. Pastor Kim is so proud of you Benjamin, as is Gonzo! I'm so longing for the day when the '3 Amigos' can ride again!

My precious wife Donna who over the years has suffered the indignity of being married to a total arsehole and erratic loon! If it wasn't for your continual nagging (encouragement) then this book would never have become reality! You are the most loving, loyal and faithful bride that a man could ever desire and I love you eternally! My 4 precious children, Natasha, Joshua, Jesse and Isaac who have suffered much as the offspring of an eccentric man, especially when their Dad was on national television for 77 days! I love you all and my pride in you grows deeper each day x.

To the Eternal God and Divine Reality by whose grace I have reached this point. Even though my mind has often strayed from You I am aware that Your love and thoughts have never strayed from me.

And to the many, many, many who have connected with me over the years, who have partnered with me, journeyed with me and invested in me, you know who you are. I love and appreciate you all x.

# ACKNOWLEDGEMENTS

A big thanks goes out to all who helped make this project happen. To those who took the time in submitting 'eye witness accounts,' you guys are awesome.

To my super intelligent family; Natasha, Joshua and Donna who all corrected my poor punctuation and grammar, and found all the right references for me, thank you.

Gary Hayes, who offered his services freely and who carefully proof-read my work, thank you. Paul and Mary Stanbury and Peter and Karen Bowen, for allowing me to use your homes as mystical bolt-holes where I felt secure, refreshed and able to put my thoughts into type. Deb Chapman who worked with me and for me as we got this book squared away and ready to send to the printers. The amazingly talented Joshua Lowe for my glorious book cover; I so appreciate your humility, patience and gifting my sweet friend. Brian Feister for allowing me to use the perfect shot of Bhawani hugging me and refusing to let go, what an awesome moment.

To all who over the years have inspired me, loved me, trusted me, partnered with me financially and journeyed with me without judgement. You guys are amazing and I'm eternally grateful for you all x.

Rather than go down the standard road of asking for 'endorsements' to validate myself and my ministry, as this is a book of stories from my life, I decided that a better option would be to have guys share their personal perceptions of moments spent with me on the road! Enjoy!

## Tim Wright

I was with Dave Vaughan on July 28, 2011 in Elmira, NY. After spending hours driving together absolutely hammered drunk, we decided to stop in at a coffee shop before the meeting that night that Dave was to speak at. As we drove closer to the place, very strange storm clouds began to form and twist together in the sky, almost in a tornado like fashion. I remember Dave yelling out with excitement in the car, "Man, this is what I've been talking about! Creation responding to the manifestation of the sons of God!"

I was just taking it all in, both Dave AND the oncoming storm before me! At the exact moment that we walked into the coffee shop, the heavens opened, I mean a torrential downpour was unleashed! It was a violent rain. You couldn't even see the parking lot through the window. It was wild! While ordering our coffee, the barista shockingly mentioned that their area had not received rain in quite a few months. She couldn't believe what she was witnessing. All Dave and I could do was laugh hysterically.

There's much more that I could write. But all of the books, at least in Elmira, wouldn't be able to hold the stories. All I know is this, my life has been forever marked by Dave Vaughan. I saw in him not only a theological paradigm big enough for the God of love and bliss that I had so desired to know in my heart, but also the ecstatic substance that he ranted and raved about! I love him for his liberty of soul, the wildness of his ideas, and the fire of his friendship!

## Shana Orser

As I write this I realise it is much more than a historic event to me. It is something that happened in me. I pray you will experience the same clarity in your heart as you read. I was with Dave Vaughan and a team in Manilla, Philippines. Once Dave arrived from South Africa we began to see lightning randomly, even without any rain or storm. We took notice. Then one evening we were ministering in a service where all the windows were opened, Dave was sharing on identity and what God believes about us. It began to rain and we could hear a distant storm, then Dave with strong conviction declared, "God worships and adores you!" Immediately the brightest flash and loudest crash of thunder followed these words. It was so obvious to everyone present that God wanted us to truly believe

these words. I do believe - God worships and adores me and He worships and adores you too!

## Peter Lowe

I was with Dave Vaughan when, in Guildford, England, that joy which is often times deemed inexpressible became expressed on the streets. The pulsating rhythms of hand drums, the dance moves and expressions that broke out mirrored the Divine as he began 'shaking His moves'. The result was that a crowd of a 150 or so gathered in the precinct.

The Hare Krishna parade passing by like an orange wave went unnoticed. the local youths suddenly began enquiring as to what was going on, seeking prayer and receiving an experiential knowledge of the love of God and receiving revelation into their lives. An airline executive received prayer after he divulged that this kind of reality is what he had been looking for. A shop assistant getting joyed up whilst in work. A lot of drunken glory all around touching hearts and lives. A rare mix of drummers, a guy in a shell suit, a monk in a wheelchair, a lady with blonde bunches singing and a random free style and break dancing troop attracted and engaged the local populace. Jesus showed up on time, NO delay. The seemingly random infused with divine purpose and extreme pleasure under a sunny afternoon sky. You Tube got hit again by the explosion of exuberant joy and 'The Nod of God' was fully embraced by those who gathered to witness the love outpouring. The rest as they say is His Story

## Nathan Kipfer

This one time I was with Dave and we were supposed to be driving to Alabama for Dave to speak. When I got in the van at my house, Dave was already trancing, the day before the weather was in the 60's outside and beautiful and not much was

forecasted to change for that day. However, it started snowing so hard that it took us almost 45 minutes to travel what usually takes 15 minutes. We were slowly moving along when all of sudden Dave 'comes to' and asks if we're near the airport. It turned out the exit for the airport expressway was coming up in the next exit or two. Dave said that he didn't think we were supposed to go Alabama and that he was supposed to go home. We drove to the airport, but no flights were available at the time. So, we spent a pleasant afternoon hanging out at the Davis' house, watching a beautiful random snow storm, and searching for the next flight deal back to the UK.

# Phil 'Homer Lad' Smith

I was with Dave Vaughan in Sheffield in 2008 when the lame walked. We were out in the city centre with a team of people and didn't really have any evangelism strategies or plan for what we were doing. We were just hammered drunk in the Holy Ghost and enjoying the Presence of God together. We ended up outside of the market area of the town centre. There were a few different local people gathered there and a guy selling cigarette lighters.

A man in an electric wheel chair came up the street towards us and although we hadn't been praying for healing or anything when I saw him it was like compassion came on me  and something in my heart said this guy should be walking. I grabbed Dave and we walked over to him. We approached him and said, "Hey, is there any chance we could just maybe pray for you to be healed?" The man selling cigarette lighters looked at us like 'here we go another couple of nut jobs.' The wheelchair guy had some friends standing next to him who started saying in Yorkshire accents, "We have never seen him walk before," and "I've known Derrick for 15 years and he's always used this

chair!" His friends didn't fill us with much confidence but we were hammered and up for anything. So we laid hands on him and felt the frailty of his body. There was no way he was going to stand up on his own, let alone walk.

Dave grabbed the arm of the electric wheel chair and lifted it up so we could get the man standing. In faith knowing that the man had no ability to stand up we helped him to his feet. He stood there swaying back and forth as we were holding him to stop him from falling over. Suddenly we could feel healing virtue leave us and hit the man's body. Dave said, "Did you feel that?!" The man's entire body was suddenly filled with supernatural strength. He immediately stopped swaying, stood straight up and filled with more shock than we had started striding up and down the street! His friends looked on wide eyed as he started shouting, "I'm walking! I'm walking!" The man selling cigarette lighters looked at us and started muttering, "Did you see that? Did you see that? I've never seen anything like that before!" The glory hit us so strongly as we just stood there laughing at what had just happened in the middle of Sheffield city centre. It was amazing!

# Gerhardt Neiwouldt

When Dave Vaughan was in South Africa with me holy chaos broke out. Heaven manifested in such a tangible way that I had to pinch myself constantly to make sure it was real! We walked in such an amazing realm of supernatural power that people around that weren't even connected to us felt the presence and were dumbstruck. We saw physical rainbows manifest, fire in our hotel room that set everything ablaze without physically damaging anything. God's glory was so intense that it took me 11 days to get out of the trance AFTER he left the country. Dave Vaughan changed my life in such a way that I can't begin to

explain. His humility, big heart and love for humanity is truly inspiring. When you have seen Dave Vaughan you have seen God!

# TABLE OF CONTENTS

# FOREWORD

In every artist, writer, creator, brewer, or believer, there always seems to be one thing that defines and sometimes even transcends their creation; that is their *story*. Andy Warhol's art wasn't just an expression of his imagination, but was his expression of his life's journey. What makes his art so meaningful and impactful is not that it is just *good art*; it's that you can see some of his story in that art. He was possibly one of the most influential modern artists in this century and made really accessible pieces that everyone could connect with; Pop art. I would assume that one reason why he desired to create pieces that resonated so well with humanity is because he probably never felt that connected as a kid. Being gay, from a Christian family, ostracized, criticized, and openly rejected, he found a way to make his heartbreak and pain into something beautiful and relatable. His way of telling his story was his art.

The great part about everyone's story is that it's not over yet, and we can still make something cherished, something precious

and something beautiful. Part of that beauty is the inability to skip to the last page and read the ending. A great ending is only as good as its journey getting there.

I'm sure that many of you that are reading this book have some sort of familiarity or history with the evangelical Christian journey. It is an honourable thing to be a part of something bigger than yourself as well as a culture that believes in morality, God, and faith, but I want to kindly suggest that maybe those are not the whole story - just pieces of it. Granted, they are very beautiful pieces - but they are just a few strokes of the grand masterpiece.

Sometimes it takes a bit of humility, and maybe even a little bit of healthy rebellion, to turn the page and read on. Wherever you are in life, faith, or theology, I can with the utmost assurance say that your journey hasn't ended. And maybe the point of all of this is not to find out exactly what or how to believe in the end - but the collective of our experiences and the life and love we shared with the people around us. Maybe the most important thing, the thing that you'll look back on when you're 80, in your rocking chair holding your great grandbabies on your knee, is not the ideology or theologies you know, but great grandpa's great story. Maybe.

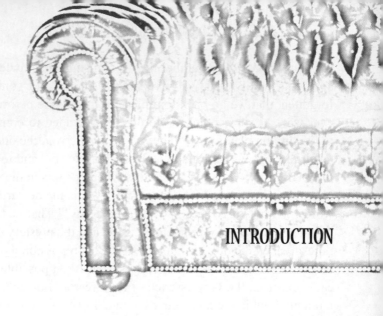

There is nothing wrong with you! You are of a Divine essence and an immortal DNA. Your origin is heavenly and stretches back to a place before time ever was. You grew up and out of an incorruptible seed and were conceived from a deep desire to be *known*. The *actual you* is perfect in every way and lacks absolutely nothing, the *pre-incarnate you* emerged from the very fabric of the creative force who formed and sustains all things. He is the One we resemble and *represent* perfectly. Made in His image, according to His likeness, formed from the very thought patterns inherent in Him for family, deeply rooted in Love (the very force of His character and nature), you were created with purpose and precision! You cannot distinguish yourself apart from Him, you cannot explain the beauty of your true self without boasting in Him, you are one with Him, always were and always will be!

For humanity to go forward we must go back, to '*remember the Rock from which we were hewn and the quarry from where*

1

*we were cut!'* Re-remembering, re-realising, acknowledging again the reality that we have always known but somehow forgotten, that we go back to a place in the Divine before time ever was. At some point in eternity you decided to come and to live life on planet earth. The *pre-incarnate you*, the one who dwelt in Him, with Him and as Him chose to 'be' and to show forth His glory. My earliest memory whether I was in the womb or whether I was a babe I cannot specify was me declaring the words "I want to go and I want to be a boy!" That statement troubled me for many years, the tension and the mystery of it at times freaked me out, how could this be? Is it possible I existed before I ever was on this planetary system? Is it possible that I came out from the very essence of the Creator Himself? Those thoughts trouble me no more, as a matter of fact I find answers and great consolation in knowing my origin, to know that we find our roots and reality firmly fixed in the Divine!

In the coming days it will become progressively more difficult for humanity to ignore it's Divinity. You are way more than you thought you were. Soon that revelation will become inescapable. What will it look like to realize you are just like your Maker? The dawning of your awakening, the reality of mankind's realization will produce alarmingly intense fruit. Effortlessly! It's crazy to think we come from a long line of gods and goddesses, those who have gone before us, who have evolved in their thinking and realized they are *one* with Divinity. I love what Stewart Brand says, *"We are as gods and may as well get good at it!"* C S Lewis touches on the Divinity of humanity in his book '*The Weight of Glory*,' in it Lewis writes the following - *"It is a serious thing to live in a society of possible gods and goddesses, to remember that the dullest and most uninteresting person you talk to may one day be a creature which, if you saw it now, you would be strongly tempted to worship. There are no ordinary people. You have never talked to a mere mortal."*[1]

1 - Lewis, C.S. The Weight of Glory (New York: Harper Collins Publishers LLC), 2001

I'll say it again, you are way more than you thought you were!

The authentic *you* is amazing and supernatural in every way. Just in *being* you have the full attention of heaven and earth. You are an *image bearer*, a carrier and a creator. You have the ability to transform and to create everywhere you go. The very substance you came from is a powerful creative force, always moving, always shifting, always causing life to manifest. You can't help but to create worlds within the very world you live, every day you act as a creator of new life! As you align with the reality of who you truly are and recognize that you are a manifestation of divine love you suddenly become the potential to shift entire regions from poverty to prosperity and from death to everlasting life. You are not just a carrier of Divinity - hell no! You are a great display, a manifestation, a full blown release of Divinity into planet earth. Nothing is impossible, nothing is beyond change, nothing around you is eternal, all things are temporal within the created order and are certainly subject to change!

All of mankind is on a journey of discovery, of coming back to our senses and of recognizing again it's true form and identity! Each journey will look different, each path is separate, even though at times paths may cross or collide. This book is my *perception* of my journey, it is my honest attempt to portray my thoughts and my experiences. Others will look at my life and have different thoughts regarding the circumstances, situations and events which I have attempted to portray within the pages of this book, that's OK, these are just *my* perceptions! In this book I use phrases which were peculiar to me at the time of experience, some of those phrases I may not use anymore or I may have moved on from. Please remember as you read this journey that this was my journey; a journey I travelled and a journey which I'm still traveling! When I talk about 'being

hammered' or 'drunk' or 'intoxicated,' these phrases were used at a time when I was attempting to give language to the experience of 'reality' which I was then beginning to engage! Some of you guys may just think of it as ecstasy, bliss or euphoria, those moments when you begin to touch a deep reality within yourself which seems beyond the norm! Many within religious circles will offer you frameworks of language and will suggest certain ideas of why and what that bliss is. Some of these suggestions may be true and some may help BUT ultimately I want you guys to remember that it's the pleasure of the wine of reality which is important and not the container placed around it!

For years people have recognized the randomness of the events in my life and for years people have urged me to get my story down in print. I am not a teacher or a theologian! If you have bought this book expecting to find within its pages some sort of accurate and flowery depiction of absolutes then you will be disappointed! The reason for me writing this book was as a means to encourage YOU and to suggest that there is a realm beyond right/wrong where reality lives, a place where we grow, learn and love! The fact that I have inserted a few 'swear words' into this book hopefully won't be too much of an issue for you, hopefully you will be gracious to me! Sometimes you just have to give vent! I also want you guys to understand that although this book contains MANY crazy and supernatural stories that in no way do I suggest that these stories endorse my theology, spirituality or the intimacy of my walk with the Divine at those points in my life!

I have had an amazing time writing this short book, I have laughed, cried and have had feathers materialize over my head and fall on me as I have re-lived and re-loved my life on planet earth! Please read, enjoy and be encouraged to live your life fully rooted in the *now*!

# Chapter One

## I'VE ALWAYS KNOWN

*"Once you were a child. Once you knew what inquiry was for.*
*There was a time when you asked questions because you*
*wanted answers and were glad when you found them.*
*Become that child again, even now!"* C S Lewis[2]

As I stood on the old School Lane I was rocked to the core of my being! School Lane was the road, the journey that I would take each day as a young lad from my home to my first school. Each day I would walk this road, usually with a head whirring with thoughts, questions and ideas. I guess that I always *knew*, I always understood deep down that there was more to *being* than what met the eye. 'Grown ups' always seemed just that; *grown up*! Life always seemed so serious, so important. So many cool things seemed to get overlooked by them because of the busyness of their day. Details which were so important to me, things that sucked me in and got the juices of my curiosity

2 - Lewis, C.S. *The Great Divorce (New York: HarperCollins Publishers LLC), 2000.*

flowing always seemed so trivial and unimportant to the bigger guys. There never seemed to be room for dreaming and gazing! It seemed to me that with *growing up*, came a deep disinterest in the small things in life. The now moments which always seemed to get my attention remained invisible to so many others. For me there was an obvious disconnection between the mystical and blurry world of a young lad and the complicated and serious, almost business like routine of those who knew best!

What I experienced that day on School Lane as a dreamy, young 8 year old boy, could easily have been missed by anyone other than a curious kid who felt a deep connection with life. This wasn't to be the last time that I would be rooted to the spot, struck mute and immobilised by awe and wonder. No, this would prove to be be just one more link in a long chain of *now moments*, of deep connections with a reality which was way too big to overlook but which seemed unimportant to so many around me. As I gazed across the rugby field adjacent to School Lane I connected with the universe in an amazing way. How was it possible that where I stood everything was calm and still, yet on the other side of the field a tornado like wind blew through the trees which was spell binding in power? It seemed impossible to me! Naturally it was so wrong, YET everything within me knew that it was so right! Instantly in the midst of manic confusion as the wind howled through the trees and my spirit was taken with it, I connected with a reality and a oneness which has never gone away! I froze, it was too much, too deep, it spoke in a language which I understood but which I also was deeply terrified of! Running home screaming with fear seemed to be the only option. No point me attempting to share this incident with the 'grown ups'!

I've always *known*. As a young boy I spent hours reasoning stuff through, I would lay on my bed wide awake for hours just considering *stuff* - "What are we doing here? If the worlds so

6

big and so full of life how did it get here? Why doesn't the world just drop out of the sky at any given moment? Who put us here?" I guess many of these thoughts were stimulated by a crazy early memory which is etched into my being and just won't go away. I'm still not sure at what point I remembered. Was it when I was born? Maybe it was when I was in my mothers womb? Who knows? It's all irrelevant in one sense, yet I remember a moment in time when I said, "I want to go and I want to be a boy!" As a child I realised that there was a point in time where I chose to come into this world! That somehow I existed in some form or another before I found my way into planet Earth and that my desire to *be* and to *manifest* was a catalyst for my incarnation! That sounds crazy, but if true brings with it eternal significance! To understand this is to understand that you are not a *mistake*. That being here right now is not an accident, neither is it the result of human desire alone nor is it a product of human error! In one sense to realise this truth is to realise that whatever the circumstances were around you being birthed into this world are irrelevant, that they are nothing more than vehicles used to ensure that your decision to 'be' was honoured and successful!

I always knew that we were all connected, I always knew that we were all one! As a boy I would spend hours on my own, the summer holidays were always the best as they ensured I had six full weeks *aside*! Wales is a beautiful country filled with rolling valleys and meandering streams. I grew up on the side of a mountain which had the sweetest pine forest planted on it. Every morning of the holidays I would set off with my old dog Patch, my rusty old air rifle and a pack of sandwiches and would just set myself down right in the middle of those fir trees. Often as I sat there thinking and drinking from life I would begin to drift in consciousness and awareness. It was so easy for me to realise the Divine connection, it wasn't something that I created but something I engaged with. It was obvious to

me, I knew, we were One. One day as I sat there I just drifted away. I expanded and grew. I connected fully with my eternal source. It was real and yet again too real. Once again I ran home screaming with ol' Patch chasing me through the forest who must of been wondering what on earth was going on!

The supernatural for me wasn't some sort of mystical happening but was Life itself! As a boy every moment seemed mystically charged and every human seemed filled with supernatural potential. I was a *dreamer*; I lived in a realm of wonder, the world provided ample opportunity for me to lose myself in Divine reality. My earliest ever dream was crazily vivid and encouraged me to go with whatever was in my heart. In the dream I watched myself walk across the mountain where I lived. Right there on the mountain was the Tardis from the Dr. Who programs, there it was, the mystical telephone box with an ability to soar through time and space! I watched with stupid intrigue as in the dream I walked across the mountain up to the Tardis and then walk inside. I remember how super excited I was as I wondered what on earth would take place next as the door to the Tardis shut and I could no longer see myself. Then all of a sudden the door to the Tardis opened and I appeared again, this time dressed as Superman and I flew straight across the mountain and out of sight! Following that dream I knew that to be fully human was to walk in supernatural reality every day. That dream opened me up even deeper to reality, a reality not to be created but to be interacted with and enjoyed to the max!

The inquiring never left me but I guess in many ways the world does an amazing job of enticing us away from the beauty of awe and wonder. The corporate consciousness manifested by a humanity blinded by greed and insecurity, deeply rooted in a lack of revelation of it's true identity hardens us to reality! My teenage years were a blur, as soon as I was old enough I left

home and disengaged from reality! The continual allure of the drug culture was strong, my desire to engage in another realm pulled hard and the crazy world of psychedelics seemed to be the doorway to spiritual freedom.

From the age of 18 to 21 I don't think there was a day where I didn't fully give myself to whatever chemical delight was on offer. I quickly found myself being embraced and accepted into a family and culture which offered so much and which allowed space for exploration. Donna and I rented a small flat at the time and the place was continually rammed with long haired and sweet-hearted journeymen. Sometimes there would be as many as twenty of us sat around listening to Steve Hillage and Yes albums, smoking the communal bong whilst all the while discussing amongst ourselves the universal issues of life! Several of these guys are no longer with us, the road broadened for some and temptation took over!

Man I loved that phase of my journey, I in no way regret allowing my heart to wander and to enjoy those forbidden fruits! It was a crazy time. I never knew where each day would take me or where I would end up, but it was a blast! The whole thing was so ridiculously wrong yet so crazily right! Somehow at the core of our community an intense love was experienced, no man felt that what he possessed was his alone, we shared everything and valued our family. There was one pub in particular that we all frequented, we would sit around the corner of the bar together and happily spend the day there smoking weed and drinking cider. The police would often visit and just stand there and watch us! They knew who we were, where we were and they seemed happy leaving us alone as long as they had us corralled into that one corner of the world. None of us owned anything, but that corner was our corner and our portion of heaven on earth. Soon enough the law caught up with me. I was found in possession of cannabis and appeared in court. I really wasn't

bothered, it was my opportunity to make a stance for freedom. At the court hearing I was asked if I had anything to say? What a stupid question, of course I had something to say! The next day the two local newspapers ran their stories, the headlines were, 'Happy day when hash is legalised,' and 'Peaceful smoker protects his sources!' GLORY!!!!

In the midst of all of the craziness and fun there will always be a paradox that manifests. Some drugs can be amazing tools of opportunity and healing if used correctly. IF they are used correctly! I experienced a lot, not all experiences were great! I remember once having a one night stand with a girl - it was wrong - she had recently broke up with a guy who was sort of a friend. He found out about our fling and decided to get his own back on me. His method of revenge wasn't to beat me up or to spread crazy, viscous rumours about me. No his method of revenge was to spike my drinks with LSD and then whilst I was flying on some crazy trip to psychologically beat on my brain! It was all arranged, I was invited to a party by friends, one drink was full of LSD which no-one drank from except me! It was a wild night of intense hallucinations and paranoia as the man and several of his friends mentally persecuted me. There was no escape. I was left deeply affected and became a nervous wreck for months after.

This was the life I signed up for, it was crazy and I saw several of my friends lose their lives to addiction and drug related incidents. Years after I evolved out of the whole thing I remember being in my local town attempting to evangelise the masses with the message of the cross! As I looked down the street there was one of my childhood friends walking towards me with a gang of his mates. We had grown up together, walked to school together, had gone hunting together and fooled around with girls together. We had both smoked our first joint together in the forest near to my home but things had massively

progressed since then. I loved this guy to bits and always will! As he walked towards me it was as if my eyes were suddenly opened to the spirit realm all around us and I saw a thick black cloud all around my friend. It was real and I knew that he was in danger, that things weren't great with him. As he came towards me I hugged on him and said, "Dude I love you so much. Please give it all up bro', you are loved endlessly and *life* has so much to offer you." He laughed, we laughed, we hugged and he just told me not to worry and he ensured me that he would be fine. Shortly afterwards he attended a party where another friend of mine injected him with a lethal dose of heroin. Sadly my friend transitioned that day! Man I hate that stuff.

It's crazy looking back that in the midst of all the wildness which I was experiencing that somehow I was still aware of my Divine reality. I still dreamed crazy dreams, still believed in the supernatural and still saw weird stuff manifest in my life. Around that time for some reason I had bought a ferret as a pet and would take it around the pubs with me. Its name was 'Ronald Citizen Biggs' it was a nasty piece of work that bit my sister several times! As I sat in a pub with a good friend one night suddenly he said to me, "Hey I like your ferret bro', I'd also like to have one." What a noble desire! Instantly for some crazy reason unknown to me I suddenly had faith for the guys desire! I suddenly heard myself spurt out the words, "What if right now the door of the pub opened and a ferret walked in, it walks over to the table and you pick it up and put it in your pocket!" What a stupid thing to say! Yep I suppose every day in pubs all across the United Kingdom this stuff happens! Yet that is exactly what was said and that is exactly what happened! As we sat there together suddenly the door of the pub opened and a ferret walked into the pub! It walked straight over to our table and my friend Andrew picked it up and put it in his pocket! (I know, it sounds weird, if this is too much for you then please don't continue reading this book, it may all get too much for

you!) Strange things like this often took place in my life, I never questioned it. For me these manifestations were a strong indication of the connection that always existed between myself and the Divine.

I also remember that around that time Donna and I went out for a night together with her family. We were at a club in an area which was unfamiliar to me. As per usual I wasn't satisfied with a 'quiet night out'! No way, things had to get hectic. No room for moderation or the exchanging of pleasantries! I hammered the booze into me all night, there was no holding back. By the end of the evening I was more than a bit buzzed and Donna and I were having a little more than a straightforward argument with each other! I stormed out of the club and decided to climb over a fence and run down a steep bank to the bottom. As I ran off I could hear Donna screaming from the road for me to go back but by this point I was fully out of control. As I hurtled down the bank with Donna screaming from the road for me to stop I suddenly hit an invisible wall. It was totally supernatural, it shouldn't have happened, momentum was propelling me forward yet I instantly stopped! As I hit the angelic wall in front of me and got rooted to the spot a train flew straight past me! I then realised that the reason Donna was screaming at me from off the road was because she knew the area and was aware that I was running headlong onto a train track with a train heading right for me! My life was spared that day by Divine intervention.

It was only a matter of time before grace overtook my life. At the age of 21 with a body filled with more narcotics than your local pharmacy shelves and a head filled with more questions than answers, I received a Divine shake up. For some crazy reason every time I would hit the local town some religious nut job would take it upon themselves to come over and talk with me. It was always pleasant enough, the only issue was that even

though they attempted to be sincere in their belief, their lifestyles were far from sincere. Most of them I knew from the pubs and bars, yes they had a theology, yes they 'sorta' believed, but their lives were messed up and if I was going to give it all up then I wanted reality. One day I bumped into a guy who I once bought my amphetamine off. For some reason he looked different, he was dressed well, seemed happy and looked in a much better place. As we chatted he shared with me that his life had been transformed, that GOD had visited him and transformed not just his life but the life of his entire family. He seemed sincere enough and his words penetrated my heart but I needed my own experience, my own encounter.

A few days later I went to visit my parents. I was back to the mountain, back to reality. I was ready for change, I sensed that my ship had run it's course and unless I jumped off now that I would soon find my life dashed to pieces on the rocks of my own recklessness. I had spent weeks in a depressed state and many days without the ability to sleep. My mind was screwed, my life and my marriage were in a mess. I was soon to have a child yet I felt like a child myself, I was immature and in need of constant care. As I left my mother's home and walked down the hill I suddenly found myself encapsulated in a bubble of Divine presence. Once again I was rooted to the spot. That same presence that blew through the trees years before, opposite School Lane, and had me rooted to the spot as a young boy now had me rooted to the spot yet again. As I stood in that bubble of liquid honey time seemed to stand still. This was a Divine moment, an eternal moment. The world hushed for those few minutes. No cars, no people, just me and God experiencing and encountering each other yet again! In that moment I knew again that He/She/It was real, that She was Love and that we were *one*. Some would call this a 'conversion experience' but I wasn't being changed or transformed into something or someone else! No this was more than that, this was a Divine re-connection. This

was a meeting again with an old and dear friend, One whom I had always known, One from whom I could never escape. I may have mentally distanced myself from Him but this was the start of being re-acquainted. Right now words fail me as I drink from that experience yet again. Some moments are beyond words.

# Chapter Two

## RELIGION KILLS, BUT THE SPIRIT GIVES LIFE

To *awaken* is an amazing thing. Those moments of realisation, knowing that you have always *been* and have always 'belonged' are priceless. To 'know' that you were always connected, that there was never any distance or separation from the God Person. To understand that you were only ever blinded to the glory of an existence which always existed and was always manifesting all around you. To begin to comprehend a reality and a God who transcends religious boundaries and racial divides, who is '*through all and in all*,' changes everything! Looking back I now realise how the Divine was never in the business of changing *me*! His/Her desire was not to make me into something that I wasn't, but His efforts were always to awaken me to a reality that lays 'within.' A reality which was always present but which I was finding hard to comprehend. It is a journey of inner discovery, of inner knowing and inner awakening to a reality more sure than any theological absolute out there! We came from Him, we are in Him, as Him. We are fully connected to the

only source of *life* and creativity in the universe and we have always had our *being* in Him!

Religion does all that it can to define, by it's own limited revelation and restricted thoughts, who and what God is. Honest men give their lives in an attempt to explain and reveal what they believe is the truth about God! Down through the ages the bold and the fearless have offered all, even their own lives, as a sacrifice in an attempt to bend the mind of man to accept *their* revelation of *their* God. All very noble stuff, yet looking back over history it's obvious that in all of their zeal to communicate *their* truth, their message was still riddled with so much mixture and error. There is no error in *awakening*. As we come to that place of *knowing* and of understanding, as our eyes are opened to the reality of Divine Love and Life, instantly our hearts know that we have always *been* and have always *belonged*. As my old pastor, Haydn Williams would say, "A man with an experience is never at the mercies of a man with an argument!"

Sadly so often at the point of realisation humanity feels the need to unnecessarily funnel it's experience straight into the dark world of religious dogmas and extremes. Instead of remaining in that place of awe and wonder, of enjoying the moment of knowing that we are loved and accepted, we seek further endorsement and look for answers via the religious systems built up around us! Religion denotes that freedom is not equated by the quantity of bliss we are experiencing but via the quality of the understanding that we possess! Freedom without answers looks like folly, religion suggests that being able to rightly communicate truth is way more important than simply experiencing life in the *now*. I was soon to understand that it's not always those who seem to have all the answers who are the ones who can aid a man in his spiritual journey. As a matter of fact I was soon to find out that it's often those who are full of certainty and *spiritual understanding* who are usually

those who have been so conditioned by religious systems that they are now failing to evolve themselves and cannot help those who are beginning to awaken around them!

In seeking a deeper understanding of my 'experiences' I looked to have them qualified via my local Pentecostal Church! For three years we attended and did all that we could to connect with their brand of spirituality. Although they dressed 'sorta' formal with the men all wearing black pin-striped suits and the ladies dressed up like a dog's dinner, they all seemed sweet enough and they were all able to speak in weird languages or 'tongues!' We got sucked in. Hook, line and sinker we signed up! Before the first year was over I was all suited up and my once hot and liberated wife was now wearing a hat to church every Sunday and was forbidden from wearing makeup or the colour red! One of my friends would always comment that the only thing that was missing from the church building was a huge glitter ball above the congregation. I mean this was more ball room dancing than ecstatic union with God!

There were so many meetings to attend. Two every Sunday. The first meeting was just for the hard core church attendees! This was the service to really show off your growing spirituality. This was your time to shine, whether it was by showing your unwavering commitment via your continual early morning attendance or by demonstrating your growth as a true Pentecostal as you first gave a simple message in tongues, then at a later date you showed your ability to interpret those tongues! All radical stuff, all necessary in the hard core world of evangelical fundamentalism! If you were really progressing well down the road of total indoctrination you may then get the chance to share a little 'word' with the congregation! This 'word' wasn't seen as a real sermon as you were yet to reach that level of spirituality, but it was your opportunity to prove that you were committed

to the cause and that you had been faithful in reading your King James Bible throughout the week! You go boy, arise and shine for your moment has come! In reality the Sunday morning service was a real pain in the backside for Donna and I. It meant we had to get up extra early, get a baby ready, walk about a mile (usually through the horrendous conditions provided by Welsh weather), whilst all the while arguing like cat and dog because neither of us (usually Donna), wanted to be there!

Sunday night was the jewel in the crown of the Pentecostal experience, as this was the Gospel Meeting. From what I can now gather the Gospel Meeting meant that a different Gospel was wheeled out especially for those who had yet to hear the *other* Gospel! This was like a mini-conference but only lasted about ninety minutes. There was always a special soloist who gave a Gospel song and the meeting HAD to end with an appeal and a call for salvation. Rarely did anyone new ever attended our little church so there was always an obligation placed upon us young ones to go forward and rededicate our lives to the Lord! This ensured the maintenance of our eternal salvation and doubled as a feather in the cap for the preacher! It showed the speaker that he was valued and that his message was still powerful because the 'altars' were half-filled with warm bodies! Man such devotion! It all helped to ensure that the system kept going and that the wheels remained glued upon the fundamental machine!

Monday was your day off! It was a great opportunity to recover from Sunday and to charge your batteries in readiness for another hectically busy church week! It was also the day where you were required to humbly meditate upon yesterdays teachings! Tuesday was the prayer meeting where eloquent men, professionals in their class, would all stand up one after the other and would each take turns in mouthing off incredible epiphanies from heaven.

Wednesday was the Waiting Meeting! I'm still not sure what or who we were all waiting for? None the less we would all gather in the home of one of the elders of the church and together we would all patiently 'wait on the Lord!' I will always remember just how crazy those afternoons were. Basically the living room where we gathered was as hot as a sauna as the open fire raged in the hearth and the atmosphere was intensely charged with an anticipation that 'something' was about to happen. It was incredibly hot in that room! The fact that we were all suited up added another dimension to an already hot and stifled situation. Man that fire burned hotter than the flames of Hell that we were all so fundamentally devoted too! The 8 of us who attended that meeting felt like a family of reptiles housed in an aquarium! The Sahara had nothing on that glory! I remember one session where the heat was so unbearable that one guy dropped off to sleep and started snoring to the dismay of the old girl who hosted the meetings! She proceeded by using her bony elbow to smack him in the ribs to wake him up! Wake up he did, with a startle and the words, "I'll close in prayer, I'll close in prayer!" It was hilarious. The stifling heat just made for a drowsy, sweaty and somewhat uncomfortable time of fellowship together. Anyways I'm sure at least God was impressed by our stupidly misguided devotion as we all nodded off to sleep in the guise of 'trancing out!'

Thursday afternoon was time for the Thursday Special - this was nothing more than a Sunday morning service penciled in for a Thursday afternoon! These meetings were geared towards those who missed out on Sunday, or for zealous individuals who felt they needed another dose of Sunday's ministry!

Friday started with the Coffee Morning! This outreach was promoted under the guise of a chilled out morning together, an opportunity to invite a few of your 'unsaved' friends and family along to 'break them in to church life!' It all sounded great but

in reality it was just another opportunity to manipulate guys into becoming just like us! Once the china cups were washed up and put back in the church kitchen cupboards the radical amongst us would then hit the local town to evangelise the masses.

Radicals we were, misguided radicals but radicals none the less! One guy spent a week creating a huge 8 foot cross which had some relevant evangelistic scripture painted under it! I will always remember that 8 foot cross which one of us would have to roll through the town and erect right outside our favourite preaching spot. We would then rig up a microphone to a mini amplifier and position it strategically to hit the old Kwik Save store across the street! We had worked out that if we positioned the amplifier correctly that the sound would have the potential to bounce from the old shop front ensuring that it would be heard in a blind spot by unsuspecting passers by! These mini preaches were great opportunities to develop skills which we would soon need once we were ready to preach at the Sunday night Gospel meetings! Our little sermonette's in town usually majored on the perils of gambling, alcoholism and drug addiction! There was never any good news preached, just a bunch of legalistic warnings aimed at those who were free enough to enjoy what we considered 'the devil!'

As I look back it's crazy to see just how much separation was in our preaching and thinking. People *outside* of our circles weren't seen as friends but more like enemies, they were more of a commodity than a community. They were *wrong*, but we were *right*. They didn't need their eyes opened to the beauty of who they had always been, hell no they needed to be transformed, to be changed and to become just like us! Whilst they were in that place of darkness they were bound to an eternal damnation and it was our *job* to *do* everything within our power to urge them to reconsider their ways and join our church! It wasn't love that compelled us but a religious system which demanded our

unwavering dedication to whatever it felt was essential in the sight of God. We had arrived, we were the elite, we were those who *knew God* and who knew exactly what He demanded of us. Can I just say that in a day where there is a major focus on Islamic Fundamentalism, that I can now see I was blindly involved in something just as dangerous - Evangelical Fundamentalism! Dangerous stuff! Run as fast from that stuff as a young man should to escape the clutches of a woman riddled with Venereal Disease!

Friday night was Faith Builders night! This was another special meeting put on to encourage guys just like me who were *immature in the faith*! By now it had already been a pretty long day and week of commitment to the cause but it would be rude not to attend a meeting especially created for *my* spiritual benefit. So show up I would, usually to the dismay of a wife who hadn't seen me all day, who had struggled away at home all by herself whilst I was out forcibly advancing the kingdom. These Friday night gatherings proved to be nothing more than theological battlegrounds. We knew it would get messy before we even arrived. The question was not *if* there would be collateral damage but just how much damage there would be, AND who this week would be the ones walking away wounded!

The continual problem was this - there were about a dozen of us who were beginning to wake up to reality! We were all beginning to realise certain things about God, ourselves and each other, somehow it all had to be filtered in and through the conditioned thinking which was solid within the religious system we had all signed up to be a part of. Something had to give. These meetings were threshing floors of pain and bloodshed, these were the levelling grounds where every high thought of disobedience to God's word was brought crashing down! Eternal matters were raised in these gatherings - will the church go through the tribulation? Did God want us to financially prosper

21

or was poverty always a plan of His to keep us dependent upon Him and Him alone? Should women be accepted in church leadership or should they remain silent, as Paul seemed to suggest? Could a Christian have a demon? Could a demon have a Christian? These were never pleasurable moments together! It was obvious that to remain in fellowship we had to conform. To conform was to grow and to develop spiritually, all the while leaving humanity in your wake! Conform we did but only for a season!

By Saturday you were not only exhausted but probably in deep trouble with your dependents who'd barely seen you all week! Every Saturday we would go out in twos, (this was the good Lord's prescribed way in the gospels, so we followed suit), knocking on doors, urging people to respond to Jesus Christ. I must admit that this little venture was probably all my fault, I'm always a glutton for having yet another plate to spin! In all of my zeal I so wanted to share my awakening with others. One day I had an idea, hey why don't I put my testimony down on paper in a non-religious way and post one through every door in my area? So I did, but this didn't seem enough. Maybe I should follow up by knocking on doors and asking guys if they read my testimony and ask them what they thought? So I did, and this started our 3 year, every Saturday morning without fail, door knocking campaign!

Over those 3 years we never failed to get reactions!! We were laughed at, shouted at, snarled at, barked at, sworn at AND once had a bucketful of dirty bong water thrown over us by a gang of drug taking teenagers! Whatever, we always prided ourselves for our zeal and willingness to go out to where the heathen Philistines were gathering to present to them an opportunity to get saved!

It wasn't all wasted energy, we did actually see some cool stuff manifest right in the middle of the drug communities of

Pontypool. Over a short period of time we saw about 30 guys, all long haired, leather jacket wearing, bong smoking, Led Zeppelin listening outcasts of society get radically hit by reality. Drug addicts, drug dealers, guys who had ran away from home at a young age all got incredibly hit by the glory of God. At one point the church started putting on buses to transport these new converts to and from the meetings. It was a fun time and we saw healing manifest in the lives of many. The only problem was the religious system! In no way was the system flexible enough to accommodate these ones who were so radically different to what they were used too. Sadly *their* Gospel wasn't inclusive enough, neither was their patience strong enough to wait for anything other than an instant transformation. So we ended up losing those who we worked so hard to win over, even though they were far from lost!

Joy, or lack of it, is an amazing indication of where we are truly at spiritually! You can dress stuff up as being necessary and important as much as you want but in reality once your joy levels drop you have to start to consider if your still on track! Religion and the onus that religious conditioning places upon you to be committed to the cause can only lead you deeper and deeper into a joyless spirituality! After 3-4 years of deep religious commitment to the system my joy dried up. It wasn't just the commitment to the gatherings that left me as dry as an old chip, it was allowing my mind to be infiltrated with thoughts and frameworks that alienated me from living life and which demanded a sacrifice which I mentally and emotionally wasn't able to produce. I would wake up at 6am every morning and for two hours would violently pray through an A4 sheet of names whose souls were in danger of hell fire! If I managed to accomplish this daily task I would be so filled with pride for the rest of the day! I seriously considered that this was a duty

given me by God and that I was the only man that He could trust with the lives of these dear ones! Man, their eternal destiny rested with ME! If I was too tired to wake up that day and pray through my list I would *so* beat myself up that I would not be able to go into my 'closet' to meet with God for days at a time! When I would re-engage the Divine I would literally crawl into the prayer room on my knees weeping, begging for forgiveness so that I could be restored to this impotent rather than important misery, I mean *ministry*! It was crazy, so wrong, such a nutty departure from an initial realisation that I was 'One with God' and that He was eternally pleased with me! Religion hey!!!

There was nothing wrong with our zeal. I mean we were burning white hot! It was just that our fiery zeal was seriously misplaced. Instead of running head long into life, intoxicated on so much ecstatic bliss that we caused transformation just in the *being*, we isolated ourselves from life in service to an austere God. Our works were not only unnecessary but also misplaced. Instead of working *from* a place of favour and *out* of a secure identity, we worked *for* favour and to *have* an identity! Our reason for living wasn't life itself. We weren't satisfied with the life that we had, so we did all we could to disengage from life and in so doing created for ourselves some sort of false world which was only relevant to those living in it! No wonder guys wanted nothing to do with us. No wonder our families and old friends thought that we had totally lost the plot and feared for our sanity! Religion is no different the world over, they honour what their traditions say are relevant and in so doing they make themselves irrelevant to all around them! A form of godliness but with no real power!

I was dry, joyless, beat up by religion and in need of a heavy dose of reality! One day I was in my prayer room and I went into a vision. In the vision I saw a stone monument made up of large boulders. It looked like a big memorial, and I had pride enough

to think that it was a depiction of Gods pleasure in my works of service! I actually thought that this monument had been erected by God in honour of my service! Then I heard a voice saying, "This is a memorial of dead works which YOU have erected! It will all come tumbling down!" I then watched as the entire thing came crashing to the ground and dissolved! Man, this couldn't be right? How could He not but be impressed with my fasting, giving, attendance, sacrifice and total dedication to church life? Then I realised I had no joy, I had no life, I was sad and had a marriage which was more of a dictatorship than a loving union of hearts and minds. Something had to change but how could I ever be freed from such a heavy and religious system?

I will always remember that each month the church would receive the *Joy* magazine, (I love irony!) *Joy* was the Assembly of God's official magazine and the denominations way of sharing to their congregations whatever news they felt relevant. I remember that around that time I was intrigued each month by the 'letters' section of the magazine. It seemed that one guy in particular was causing something of a stir. He was a South African preacher residing in America by the name of Rodney Howard Browne! Each month I would read intense letters aired in the magazine regarding Mr. Browne and the meetings that he hosted. One month a Pastor would write saying that Rodney had visited his church and that the church had been totally transformed! The next month there would be a letter from some big religious organisation who would come out in saying that Mr. Browne was 'of the devil' and that they would be praying for his influence and his meetings to end, encouraging all to stay away from the man. I was intrigued by all of this, it got my attention, my curiosity was awakened! Then one month I saw an advert right there in *Joy* magazine: 'Rodney Howard Browne will be hosting a week of meetings at Earl's Court, Olympia,

London, December 1995. Register Today!'[3] Instantly I knew I had to go, this had to be the way out, the way back to bliss? I signed up!

3 - Joy Magazine (Nottingham: New Life Publishing Co.), 1995.

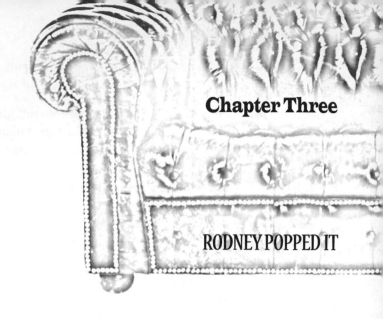

# Chapter Three

## RODNEY POPPED IT

There have been a few moments in my life when over a short space of time everything changed. Times where I look back and I realise that from that moment on nothing would ever be the same again. Times where I have changed, and a new realm of reality opened to me which never seemed to close again. Moments where I have known that the toothpaste has been squeezed out of the tube and there's no way of putting it back in. We have all had these times, moments where something registers in the depth of your being, where you see something and you know that you will never again be able to 'un-see' it. Times when you are marked indelibly and eternally and are changed into another person. Just like Saul on the road to Damascus, where you are hit so hard that you are blinded by a reality which leaves you with a new name and a new identity. It's not that you become something that you weren't, it's just that by experience you begin to manifest something of what you have always been! The *true you* get's revealed, and the false, egotistical *you* gives way to truth. I've experienced those moments and will share

about those crazy times over and over in this book. This week was just one of those times, so get ready to be rocked!

As the bus trundled along it's way to London myself and my buddy Paul, (some will know him from my YouTube video 'two drunk pirates,' - The Apostle Paul Watkins[4]) were left alone with our thoughts. It was a massive gamble for us, we were leaving the safety of our religious environment in the face of fierce opposition to seek out a man whom we knew nothing about. All I knew was that my joy had dried up and that my connection with the Divine who had once revealed himself powerfully to me just a few years back was feeling more distant than ever before. Whatever bliss I had known, whatever fire of love once burned within me, religion had done a great job of quenching.

As I sat on that bus with tears streaming down my face I heard myself saying, "I have to know that connection with you again. I feel dry, I have sacrificed everything yet it has got me nowhere. If you don't touch me again I will go back to my old life, all of my old friends are living more pleasurable lives than this". There was no answer, it was one of those moments when you realise that maybe, just maybe you've totally ran your course and that this possibly could be the end of it all.

We arrived in the United Kingdom's capital of London to be greeted by freezing temperatures and a sweet friend who once attended our small church back in Pontypool. Lynne's family all worshipped with us but she had moved away and now lived in Harrow, London. Lynne rented a small flat and was keen for Paul and I to stay with her there whilst we attended the conference. I was gifted with the living room sofa and Paul the cold hard floor! We went to bed that night wondering, so many what if's? This whole thing was going to go one of two ways, we were committed now and there was no backing out! The meetings

4 -https://www.youtube.com/watch?v=XSPP46d4n38.YouTube "2 Drunk Pirates Take 2"

started the following day and we were up bright and early to catch the Tube to Earls Court.

We were already pretty nervous when we showed up the following day for the start of the conference, I mean who was this guy? Why was there such a stir about him? What were these crazy manifestations that so many seemed to have so many issues with? Those early nerves were added too as we arrived at the hall and right outside the building stood about fifty people waving placards and banners urging people not to enter through the door to the conference! The protestors seemed friendly enough and were obviously other Christians whose angst against Rodney seemed to focus upon the evils of the 'strange fire and wine,' which apparently Rodney was offering his congregants. Weird, I had no understanding at all of what they were talking about, but hey it all added to the atmosphere. As we walked into the hall I realised straight away that this was different! The little church I attended would pull in an average of 25 folks on a Sunday night, maybe if we hosted a special event we would have 70 show up! This place was rammed with thousands of people from all over the world, this was somewhat different. Added to all of that our little church worshipped using an organ on a Sunday morning and a piano on a Sunday night, but man these guys had a full band set up AND they seemed happy!

When the meeting started I was obviously more of a spectator than a participator. I mean we had a week of this, three meetings each day, no point rushing in, I mean I don't even know this guy and maybe the protestors had a point? The worship was a blast even though it was way more lively than what we were used too, I liked it even though I felt a little intimidated when they asked for any type of extra interaction. It was all good and I felt comfortable enough. Then Rodney appeared. To me he looked about 5 foot 5 inches tall and about 5 foot 6 inches wide! The guy was 'sorta' square in shape and initially didn't seem to

smile a lot! He just paced back and forth mimicking the walk of an Arctic penguin whilst rolling his thumbs around each other! "Thank you Jesus, thank you Jesus, thank you Jesus, thank you Jesus," was about all he could muster. It all seemed biblical enough and in all fairness he seemed like a decent bloke. What did get my attention was that every now and again someone would burst out laughing - this was weird and I wasn't sure if they were laughing at Rodney or with Rodney. The little church which I belonged to spoke a lot about *joy*, so I realised that this was part of the Pentecostal experience even if it all seemed a little loud and maybe excessive! It was all going great, then someone started running around the building and Rodney saw fit to join the guy! The two of them sprinted around the hall as the congregation laughed uncontrollably!

It all seemed like great fun and all added to the intense carnival atmosphere which I wasn't too put off by. I just kept looking at Paul with an expression on my face which said, "I have not got a clue what on earth is going on here dude!" One thing which did catch my attention (in the midst of lots of things catching my attention) was that frequently through that first session guys would suddenly stand up and storm out of the meeting. At times a whole row of guys who had obviously all travelled together to the event would suddenly stand up and walk out. One time a whole bunch got up and left whilst Rodney shouted something at them about, "Don't let the revolving door slap you in the back of your head you ugly thing!" That seemed a bit rude. Before we knew it the first session was over and we left for a coffee more confused than when we arrived. It was all a bit unusual but one thing I couldn't get away from was the deepening sense of 'presence'. That same presence which I experienced on 'School Lane' all those years before was definitely here at this event. Something was happening.

Over the next couple of days we 'sorta' remained spectators

although we were starting to understand the flow of the meetings. Rodney would walk to the pulpit, take the microphone and by his own admission would go 'a-hunting religious cows!' He would then use his sermon to apply as much pressure as humanly possible in an attempt to topple fundamental idols in our thinking. He constantly mocked man's efforts to produce anything via his own spiritual services. Fasting, prayer, worship, sacrificing time from family and loved ones in the name of the *Lord*, all got exposed and scrutinised! Man this guy was as blunt and as aggressive as a smack between the eyes with a heavy baseball bat. He would label guys, "You ugly ugly thing," and would accuse them of being, "So narrow minded," that they, "Could look through a keyhole with both eyes!" He said that their, "Faces were so long you could eat oats out of the tail pipe of a car!" This guy certainly wasn't out looking to make friends or to catch favour with local churches! How can you get along with people when you tell them that they, "Look like you've been baptised in pickle juice?" This guy was an obvious abrasion to the system. At times it was hard to watch as clash after clash took place between Rodney and the religious fraternity. Looking back I now realise that the church needs many Rodneys, that in a day where guys are keen to not offend others, as it may ruin their chances of further invites, that we still need many table turners and truth talkers!

The whole thing was bizarre and as the week went on more and more people left and those who remained got wilder and looked a whole lot stranger! The manifestations disturbed me! All of my religious buttons were getting pushed - Mmmm rammed in! Guys barking like dogs and strutting like chickens, one woman having some sort of orgasmic delight laid out on the chairs right opposite me! I wanted some of this stuff controlled but Rodney had already strictly warned the ushers to touch no-one saying, "This is the operating table of the Holy Ghost, you have no idea what is going on in these people's lives. God is at work, leave

31

Him to do what only He can!" He seemed to have countless testimonies to support these suggestions, many actually. Stories of guys whose lives were radically transformed after falling under this great power, churches turned upside down after such strange encounters with the Divine! I was open, I was desperate, I just needed change!

About three days in I got whacked! It's ironic actually as it was the one session where Rodney rested and allowed some of his friends to share. It's crazy what can happen as we take our eyes off of man. I see this stuff all the time in church circles, it's like some kind of idol worship, usually based around those who are successful in ministry. Young guys who are so desperate to climb the ladder of ministerial success that they will brown nose anyone who has an ability to give them a hand up. Ministerial clones who lose their own identity and suddenly look like, sound like and preach like whoever it is they are sucking up to. I hate that stuff, probably because I'm beginning to realise that this whole global awakening is so much bigger than any man, ministry or denominational structure.

All over the earth guys are beginning to wake up. This isn't the work of a man, no this is the very pleasure of God in drawing all men to Himself and making known to His creation that we are and have always been One. It's amazing what happens when we take our eyes off of man, when we stop demeaning ourselves and our ability to hear for ourselves, when we begin to realise that we can trust that inner knowing, that thing which we often call *perception*. I'm now having guys contact me from the New Age communities, from the Islamic communities, from all different types of spiritual, racial and social backgrounds and they are all saying the same thing to me, "Dave I'm seeing it, I'm waking up!" Many of these guys would never darken a church door but seemingly there is a God who is big enough to reveal Himself to all!

Let's not take our selves too seriously here or become so spiritually bigoted that we think that the weight of global transformation is weighing upon our shoulders! I love the analogy of the little 2 year old lad who every day goes out to *help* his father who is building an extension on their family home. The father so wants the child to feel included in the build that he gives the young lad his own rubber hammer and plastic trowel, he also puts a little hard hat on the child's head just so he could be one of the team. Each day the young lad goes out onto the building site with his Pa and feels fully part of the construction process! Months later when the whole build is complete the father puts his arms around the young lad as together they look at the beautiful new extension. The son then looks up at the father and with his chest puffed out with pride says, "We did a good job didn't we dad," and the father replies, "Yes we did son, yes we did!" This is the Lords doing and it's marvellous in our eyes! He/She so wants us to feel involved and to feel included, yet ultimately it's Her hands that do all of the work!

In the afternoon session as yet *another* offering was received - which offended every ounce of my being - *it happened*. For three days I had watched pretty much everyone get 'hit,' but what about me? As I walked forward to the offering bucket I heard that inner voice say to me, "Put your hand in your pocket, take out everything that's in there and throw it in the bucket." As I responded and turned to walk back to my seat I got hit, my legs buckled, I hit the floor and instantly I felt hammered drunk. For over two hours I laid there laughing uncontrollably, all the while finding myself tangled around a complete and utter stranger! I had never met this guy but as we talked later that day I found out that he actually only lived about ten minutes from my hometown! Man it felt so good. I felt as if I was having

a full blown Holy Ghost enema, a flushing away of all the religious bullshit I had taken on board over the years. Every time I attempted to peel myself away from the floor I realised that I couldn't! My legs felt like they had lead weights attached to them and I felt as if a 25 stone angel was sat right on top of me! That was it, I had been infected, I had taken the pill and there was no going back.

The next few days were beautiful. Everything seemed right! This experience was a joy unspeakable and was full of glory. I was full, I was actually so full of sweet wine that I could actually taste it and smell it! I was drunk and man it felt good. Every care left, nothing seemed to matter, nothing seemed an issue, all I knew was that I didn't want this feeling to ever leave me! In the day we would be at the meetings and when we left at night we would have breakouts of intense reality back at Lynne's flat. I remember one of the meetings in-particular. As we stood there and worshipped together there was a crazy 'hushhhhhh' which came through the building. Suddenly we were stilled and all stood silent with our arms raised to heaven. As we stood there in total silence suddenly it felt as if the ceiling was ablaze with supernatural life and it was slowly descending upon us! The fear in the room at that moment was crazily intense, this was God but not how I remembered Him! I mean this wasn't the baby Jesus meek and mild sucking milk from His mama's teat and cooing like a turtle dove! No, this was different. The fear was so strong in that room as His presence dropped that chairs started to suddenly clatter all around me as hundreds of people attempted to clamber out of their rows and flee from the building. Rodney started shouting, "don't run, don't run, this is your Father, He loves you!" Somehow I managed to remain in my seat and I found myself engulfed in the greatest baptism of Love that I had ever experienced. I was home!

I had been transformed. I was continually, spiritually, drunk! It

felt amazing and would strongly manifest at all the wrong times. It was ODD - 'Open Displays of Drunkenness', - ODD! No matter where we found ourselves this crazy intoxication would suddenly start to bubble up. Shops, restaurants, public toilets, made no difference, this thing was no respecter of persons or situations. There seemed to be a connection between the wine on the inside and the Spirit world on the outside? I now understand this concept of the 'wheel within a wheel', the reality that the kingdom without resonates via the kingdom within, but back then I had no understanding of the direct connection between the kingdom within and the spirit realm without. It seemed that the greater the intensity of wine manifesting inside of us the more stuff began to manifest all around us. To some within the church this would have looked like absolute foolishness and I now fully understand why that would be the case! Yet these cynics would be the same religious nuts who were striving and straining each day in the prayer closet, distancing themselves from family and friends whilst all the while producing NOTHING! Man there was no going back to that life. I had tasted and seen that the Lord really was good and that His joy was a supernatural strength not to be taken lightly! There was no going back to squeaky shoes, pin striped suits and long faces! Enough was enough!

I have to tell you about the evenings that we spent back at Lynne's flat! Each night we would leave the meeting absolutely blasted and would take a Tube ride back to Harrow to sleep at Lynne's. Somehow in one of the meetings I managed to catch one of Rodney's worship CD's that he threw out, so each night we would put on the disc, lay down and basically laugh ourselves to sleep. One night as we laid there with an intensity of glory in that room the like of which I had never experienced before as all of a sudden a bright light came into the room and lit up the entire place! Paul and I just put our hands over our faces and screamed wondering what on earth it was! It was the brightest light I had ever seen, brighter than a million suns and easily able

to blind us with it's intensity! The next night as we laid there with that same electric atmosphere charging the whole flat Paul and I just looked at each other as there appeared to be someone sat on the chair right next to us! Neither of us could see anyone or anything but for an hour we sat in silence staring at the chair as it was obvious to us that we were not on our own!

On the last night at Lynne's something happened which I will never forget. Paul was asleep on the floor and I was just laid on the sofa drinking in the intensity of Love which was manifesting strong in the room. Suddenly as I laid there I heard the front door open in the flat, I wasn't spooked by this as I thought that it was probably just Lynne coming in from work. Then the door opened into our room and someone walked in and stepped over Paul and stood above him right in front of me. As I opened my eyes and looked there stood over me was a huge 8 foot angel who was just looking straight at me! I totally freaked out and I suddenly felt myself sinking deeper and deeper into the sofa. The angles face looked like it had been chiseled out of stone, he had features, a chin, nose, cheeks and the deepest blue eyes, but his face looked like stone? He had long ringlet blonde hair like tubes hanging down to his shoulders, (I call it a him but actually it was a him and a her!) There was no emotion in its face at all, I wasn't sure whether the angel was happy or sad and more to the point I wasn't sure whether he liked me or whether he was angry with me? Soon he vanished and I was left wondering what on earth had taken place!

I once talked with Jeff Jansen about this encounter, Jeff said that he had also seen a similar angel and had asked the prophet Bob Jones about it. Bob told him that these were 'Watcher Angels,' and were not to be taken lightly! When something like that happens to you the experience leaves you marked! You are left in a state, a realm of awe and wonder. From that moment on I felt as if I was actually carrying something new in my life, at

random times I will feel the presence of that angel with me and I will remember that moment of encounter.

Our week was almost up. Rodney decided to extend the meetings by a day and they moved location to Kensington Temple for one last blast. We had great seats that night right next to the stage and by this point we were ready for anything. That night Rodney asked a clarinet player to get up and perform a solo. I will always remember that moment, it was crazy. As the guy played the song 'Great is thy faithfulness,' it was as if the very glory of God was coming out of his clarinet and was filling the entire building! Man it was so intense and so real. As the guy finished playing a complete silence filled the room as the presence of God invaded so strongly. As Rodney spoke that night I burned! It was as if liquid fire was being poured upon me over a 3 hour period! The fire started on my head and slowly burned right through my entire being. As the fire burned upon me my spirit was disconnected from my body and I found myself lifted up to the rafters of the auditorium from where I watched every moment from high above. Every word that Rodney spoke that night pierced my heart, It all made sense, it all impacted me. I had vision after vision of the present awakening. I saw people from all over the world waking up, realising who they were, knowing that they were Divine just like their *source*! For 3 hours I was struck mute, the weight of glory was so heavy that I couldn't move or speak even if I wanted to.

When it was all over Paul helped me up and we headed for the Tube ride back to Lynne's for the very last time. The glory on us that night was strong, intense and seemed super charged! As we got on the train that night for some crazy reason it was rammed with commuters, apparently a train had derailed somewhere else so our train had to take extra passengers. The carriages were full of suited businessmen all late to get home. After about five minutes I looked up and I realised that everyone on the

tube was looking straight at us! Why? Then a man came over to me and with tears running down his face asked me where we had been and what was going on. At that point my tongue was loosed and I blurted out, "What you are feeling right now is the glory of God, God is real, He loves you and always will!" The man replied, "If God loves me then ask him to heal my dying Gran who's terminally ill with cancer!" We prayed together and the man just wept as we spoke life to him and his Gran. It was a crazy moment and all the while everyone else on the train looked over at us transfixed by the glory of God! No-one said a single word. This was new, this was different!

# Chapter Four

## SPIRITUALITY BEYOND RELIGION

Everything within me burns to see something of an authentic, organic and natural release of glory into Life. When I look at the church structure these days far from seeing something that is authentic and natural I see something rather unnatural and sadly disconnected from ordinary, every day life. In many ways the church has become a surrogate, something synthetic and unrealistic. To me this weird expression of spirituality portrayed by the church seems unsustainable and a strange hybrid which lacks flexibility! What myself and my friends experienced over an 18 month period starting in December 1995 was without doubt an unprecedented explosion of organic *life*. This *life* was enjoyed by a community of ex-drug addicts now turned wide eyed wonder junkies, who understood very little about what they were experiencing but who knew they had been graced to experience something way greater than their ability to produce it! Far from feeling the need to disengage from life, this whole thing broke out right in the midst of life itself. There was no escaping it, no denying it and no stopping it!

The moment that Donna opened the door on my return to Wales I fell to my knees in floods of tears. While I was away I began to realise just how badly I had treated her. In all of my spiritual enthusiasm, with all of my attempts to please God and to draw near to Him, I had distanced myself from my wife and had treated her more like an acquaintance than a lover. My attitude had been so wrong and this was highlighted to me by God whilst I was away. (The Divine has such an amazing way of correcting us whilst making us feel ecstatically joyful as He does so!) As I asked for forgiveness I realised that this was a fresh day and that we had been granted a new start together. A new foundation had been laid in our lives. Gone was the frustration, the striving and the straining to reach out to God by religious means and in came the love, joy and bliss of knowing that He is never far from anyone of us! This new foundation changed everything for us. Effortlessly every day the glory of God would break out. We would go to bed drunk, would wake up drunk and all day long we would soak in that drunken intoxication!

The Sunday after my return we went back to our little church. It didn't take us long that day to realise that whatever it was that we were now carrying didn't fit back into that religious box. In that Sunday morning gathering there was a message in tongues given and an interpretation which started with the words, "This day I have brought to you the New Wine of the Holy Ghost, but you are a stiff necked people and you refuse to bend down to drink it!" This seemed so right, we had returned home filled to overflowing with new wine but the wineskin was having great difficulty accepting this reality! Rodney had said to us whilst we were away, "You will go back to your churches and all those old ladies who sit on their favourite seats wearing their little halos will suddenly change and manifest who they truly are. You will watch as the halos disappear from their heads and horns take their place!" It seemed hilarious when he said it but in that meeting we saw that word fulfilled as person after

to create a unity, we were simply enjoying the bond and unity of the spirit which is continually in place! It was effortless!

Donna and I would be sat in our living room and suddenly there would be a knock at the door and a couple would come in, then another knock and another couple, then another, then another, until finally we would all be sat there looking at each other in amazement. It was as if an invisible force had drawn us together, this was supernatural at the core and beyond us! As we would gather together we would talk about what we had experienced that day and as we would share our hearts the glory of God would start to fill the room and together we would go into trances and visions until sometimes 3 or 4 o'clock in the morning! Friends would crawl out of our home in a crazy drunken mess and Donna and I would go to bed! The next day we would be sat in our home and I would say to Donna, "Hey let's go and visit Neal and Sarah." So we would walk to their home only to find half a dozen people already there, then a few more would arrive and then a few more! We would all look at each other in amazement and then as we would begin to talk about what we had all experienced the night before suddenly the glory would manifest and we would all go into trances and visions of God! This same pattern lasted every day for 18 months!

This was heaven, this was reality, this was as great as any revival I have ever read about, yet it was contained to a group of about a dozen of us. We would see angels, guys would get pulled into heaven and have visions, sometimes the sounds of angelic choirs or instruments would be heard, it all had a sound to it and it all synchronised perfectly with our lives! Sometimes pillars of wind or fire would manifest in the room. This wasn't a visionary thing, this was substance, this was reality. One day I sat in my living room with Donna asleep in the bedroom directly above me the glory just started to appear in the room. It was crazy. To

start with I just felt a real heat on my chest that seemed to push me back into the chair, then after a while I found myself totally sank into and felt one with the chair! Then what appeared to be a fine silver mist started to physically manifest in the room. That same mist got thicker and thicker until eventually a deep, physical cloud filled the entire room that was so dense that it stopped me from being able to see my television! As the cloud manifested I so wanted Donna to come in and enjoy this crazy experience with me, perhaps I just wanted a witness as I knew guys would have a hard job believing what was taking place in the room? I thought, "Maybe I should call Donna, she's just above me, maybe she will come down?" Then I thought again, "If I call and shout maybe the cloud will disappear and I'll be left on my own with no glory cloud and an angry wife who I just woke up for no apparent reason?" So I decided to shelve the idea and enjoy the cloud all to myself!

These things weren't encounters but life, our life had become the encounter! One day a friend came to visit me and as we sat there in the glory my phone rang and there was a distressed voice on the other end of the line. It was a friend; a friend who sometimes struggled with lust who would occasionally go and do things which he knew that he shouldn't. Each time he would fall he would beat himself up and become suicidal as a result. Here he was on the phone asking for my help, he had once again fallen and was once again feeling suicidal. I told the guy to hang fire and ensured him we would be with him shortly. As we got to his flat I remember how heavy the glory was that we carried there with us. As we sat down with the man we simply told him that he was loved and forgiven and that he just needed to forgive himself. Then as we sat back to relax all I can remember is how the ceiling became like a blazing fire and it dropped on us! Before we knew it we were consumed, we were ablaze. The whole room was on fire and there was no way of switching it off! I remember looking at my watch as the fire hit and it was

11.10pm. The next thing I knew I was in the spirit realm and I was seeing stadium after stadium in the UK filled with people and each stadium was ablaze with the fire of God. I knew in my heart that the same Spirit and fire burning in those stadiums was the same Spirit and fire which burnt in our room. I then heard a voice saying, "My people need to re-align their thoughts because I'm gonna shake this nation!"

At that point I felt myself being physically shaken by someone and as I looked up the guy whose flat we were in had hold of my arm and was saying, "Dave you have to go home now, look at your watch," I replied by saying, "Dude the glory of God is here, I am ablaze!" The man just looked at me saying, "I know bro' but look at your watch you need to go." It felt to me that we had been there just five minutes, but when I looked at my watch it was now 2.20am and we had been there over 3 hours! As we left his flat scratching our heads in amazement at what we had just encountered we turned the corner outside his flat and it was as if an angel stood waiting around the corner for us and it hit us straight across the head with a 2-by-4 from heaven. Instantly myself and my friend hit the ground and started to do all that we could to crawl up the road! I will always remember watching my friend on all fours attempting to crawl up a hill as I headed off in one direction and him in the opposite direction! I finally reached bed at around 4am saying to Donna, "You have no idea what just took place!"

It was revival, but revival for just a few of us. We had tasted something, the toothpaste had been squeezed out of the tube and there was no way of putting it back in! For a season our lives seemed to be governed by a different realm and somehow the Divine was intrinsically involved in everything that we did. Every day seemed arranged for us and every day seemed perfect. We were blessed beyond measure and knew it. We had no understanding or explanation to offer, this whole season

was more about wonder and mystery than great theology. This manifestation seemed to be the fruit of encountering Divine reality, the full bliss of an eternal connection with the source. All effort to generate or to maintain spirituality was gone, this wasn't about works but about rest. Yet weirdly we were seeing more fruit manifest than all of our striving ever managed to produce!

# Chapter Five

## HE'S WITH YOU IN THE TOUGH TIMES TOO

For 18 months we saw an unprecedented explosion of the glory of God. Every day without fail we encountered Him. It was effortless and was all just an extension of normal every day life! The detox from religious service was not only necessary but extremely blissful to not *have* to perform, show up or whip something up released us from so much pressure. Once that pressure goes life becomes what it should be, an ecstatic human encounter with planet earth. We were beginning to realise that there was a place for spirituality outside of the Christianity that we once knew and served so well. This seemed impossible to accept for a while, the freedom to flow in life apart from the church structure was difficult to embrace. There was continual pressure placed upon us by those who we once fellowshipped with to *attend* and to gather, we *were* gathering and were experiencing supernatural life together, it just wasn't within that stereotypical church setting. Whenever we attempted to share with others the glory of our new spiritual dynamic they always frowned upon our encounters and freedom because it

didn't fit within what they knew. It was obvious that what was more important to them was that we conformed to the known path and that we had some sort of 'spiritual covering' over us! For crying out loud we were probably experiencing more together than anyone had in our nation for decades! Pillars of fire, clouds of glory, spontaneous joy outbreaks on the streets, lives radically transformed and changed forever, yet it was not enough for a system that loved and demanded human sacrifice!

I suppose over time we got ground down by it all. After all we were disconnected from mainstream Christianity, there was no structure to our meeting together and yes apart from the great Holy Ghost and the God of all creation we were lacking a religious covering in our lives! As a group we decided to join a local church that had previously been hit by the 'Toronto Renewal' a few years previous. It was the only church that we knew of in our area which 'sorta' walked in the spirit and were seemingly saying the right stuff. We went with a plan that to appease others we would attend and be a part of the Sunday services BUT agreed that we would continue to flow with whatever it was that we were currently experiencing in our homes. This sounded great but in practice was soon shown to be a flawed experiment. It didn't take long for us to realise that whenever the wine flows in a new way that it will never be able to flow within an old wineskin or structure.

We quickly caused problems and soon blew stuff up! It was obvious that whatever we were carrying was an obnoxious and irritating abrasion to the religious system. It wasn't long before the leaders started to meet with us individually! We were encouraged with strong 'prophetic words' and other divisive and manipulative means to stop meeting together and to start spending less time with each other! I was seen as the 'leader' of this unruly pack so was quickly labeled as a trouble maker and some sort of cult leader. The guys knew that this wasn't the case

but I suppose over time you get worn down and it's easier to accept a lie than hold to the truth. So sad. The congregants were also told to keep away from us and were encouraged to not have us enter their homes! This led to some awkward moments when I went to visit people and was left standing outside without being offered an explanation of why I wasn't being invited in as usual!

Things would get messy every time a guest speaker would show up. It would be pretty obvious that preachers would be *briefed* before the meetings and that I would be highlighted as a rebellious, religious nut, who needed to get delivered of devils! One guy came to visit and as I went to shake his hand after he preached he looked at me and said, "Something was highlighted to me today. You have an anointing the size of a double decker bus BUT unless you repent God is going to take you out! He will kill you!" I was instantly aware that unless I refused those words that they had the potential to mess me up! I mean God's gonna kill me? So I replied with, "You've been listening to the voice of man and not the voice of God, what you have said is a lie and will not come to pass!" (Twenty years later I'm doing better than ever and at the gym today I set a new bench press personal best of 120KG for 7 reps, BOOM!) The church was riddled with this stuff, weird shit, strange fire. All foolish manipulation coming out of fear and insecurity, the fruit of never knowing that we are Love and of walking in the freedom of that Love.

It must have been obvious to them that we were carrying something special, the glory on us was so strong and we were so happy. Sometimes as I would be driving to the church I would suddenly become aware of everything which would take place in the meeting that day before I even turned up. One Sunday as the worship came to an end I took the microphone and started prophesying, "The anointing oil is about to flow in this place.

You have been called and today will be appointed. As the oil hits you today know that this is a new day of leadership for you." The next thing I know the Pastor calls out two couples from the congregation, he pours oil over their heads and starts praying over them and setting them in as Elders in the church! (Little did I know that over the weekend the old leadership left the church and that the Pastor was setting new leaders into place that day!) This stuff would happen all the time, yet it seemed that it was overlooked as I was the rebellious kid who needed to change. It didn't take long for whatever was happening with us as a group to diffuse and for us to just be left once again with form, tradition and a religion that lacked power.

The spiritual abuse at times was so heavy. As I would sit in the congregation it seemed that wave after wave of spiritual attack was coming against me. I'm not talking here devils and demons and horned creatures with pitchforks laughing and prodding me! No I'm talking about the affect and the power of words spoken by a creative force, sent like fiery barbed arrows straight into your soul. It hurt. Often I would leave the meetings devastated, I would walk into my home with tears streaming down my face and would start to be physically sick because of the weight of the words which had been spoken over me. I spiritually crumbled. All of that sweetness of 18 months of continual encounter was gone, I felt awful and ashamed that I had let something so precious leak from my life. To know that I had been seeing something so outrageously God manifesting in my home which others hadn't seen for decades and all that now remained was hurt and pain was way too heavy for me to carry. I left the church, should never have gone!

I needed something to take away the pain and to fill the hole in my life. I had to switch off and to try and forget what I had lost or else it was all too much to bear. I always had an interest in hunting, from a young age I would go shooting and loved

being outdoors. So I bought myself a lurcher (Saluki crossed with a Greyhound,) and I started going hare coursing with a bunch of gypsy lads who lived local to me. I loved and I still love the gypsy community, that pace and way of life always seemed so appealing to me, traveling the countryside with your family, hunting and living from the land, the universe providing it's bounty for you. Amazing! I've also always had an unusual interest in people who are different, I love characters, personalities, 'one of a kinds'! That's probably the reason that I detest the whole cookie cutter, Christian cloning system which is rife within the church these days. These gypsies were certainly different! I couldn't understand much of what they were saying BUT they were different and they knew all the best places to go hunting! I loved visiting them and sitting in their caravans, we had some crazy conversations together usually over a nice cup of tea in their best bone china cups! They were certainly different, but man I love different!

About 3 times a week I would get a knock at the door by my gypsy brothers usually right at the time Donna and I would be settling down for the night, "Brother David do you fancy going out tonight for a spot of coursing! It's a beautiful night Brother David and I'm sure that the good Lord Himself will want us to have some sport!" (They loved bringing 'our Lord' into stuff whenever they wanted an endorsement to their request!) I usually went, it was rude not to, I was part of the team, these were my new friends, pretty much my only friends! Night after night we drove to the rolling hare filled fields of the Cotswolds found right in the heart of England. The drive was almost two hours long, so to kill time we would usually find ourselves singing gypsy songs and sharing stories of elusive hares who escaped capture. We would then rock up on someone's ten thousand acre estate late at night with no permission and more stealth than 007! We were poachers and dare I say pretty good at it, although evading capture was paramount! Fines were big and shotguns

nasty! We did get caught once and Tewksbury magistrates court issued me with an £80 fine for 'destroying a rabbit on Dibden Lane!'

All would be great on the drive to England but then the arguing would start usually over whose dog caught the hare! One would say, "My dag caught that hare," the other, "No, my dag caught that hare." Then it would escalate too, "I wouldn't feed your dag, it's not worth a shilling!" That would be countered with, "Your dag couldn't catch a hare in a barber's shop, it couldn't catch a hare in a phone box!" Then we would find ourselves heading back to the van for a long drive home and the conversation now turned too, "That's it now Brother David we are never going again. I swear on me old Granny's grave Brother David that's the last time. We are never going again Brother David!" All seemed sincere enough until the following night when there would be a knock at my door and as I opened it I would be greeted with, "Brother David do you fancy a great night's coursing tonight? The good Lord is with us and tonight we will kill many hares!" I would always ask the question, "I thought we weren't going anymore?" And would always be told, "The good Lord told us to forgive Brother David, we have let bygones be bygones!" That was always the way and I loved it all!

I loved the hunting but it was pretty obvious that something major was missing in my life! I started attending a pretty big charismatic church near to me where in all fairness stuff seemed to be happening. I would show up a few times a month but it all seemed so tame after what we had been experiencing together. The hurt and disappointment on the inside of me ran deep. I needed help and I knew it. One day at the church the Pastor said, "Today I'm going to speak about a God who can heal any wound, even the wounds that a doctor can't heal." As he spoke I felt that hurt pulsating on the inside of me, the fruit of hundreds if not thousands of negative words and suggestions launched at

me from the pulpit. As the pastor finished speaking he asked if all the prayer team could come forward and stand at the front of the hall. He then asked all those who knew they needed some sort of healing to walk forward. It was a 'no brainer'! As I walked out a guy made a beeline for me and just hugged me tight to himself. As he hugged me it felt as if a torrent of all those hurtful words suddenly gushed up through my being and left me as I let out a crazy howl. I left free that night, emotionally free. The hooks of control were gone, all of those false attachments were severed. I was free but still felt distant from the God whom I loved.

It doesn't matter how distant we feel we are One with the Divine. He is closer to us than the very air that we breath. There is no distance, there is no separation, even though we may feel that there is. He is Love and He continually draws us into that sense of closeness with His Cords of Love. He was drawing me again. Around that time I worked shifts in a factory which produced brakes for cars. Pretty ironic really as it was obvious that the spiritual brakes had definitely been applied in my own life! I would work all sorts of crazy shifts and would see all sorts of crazy supernatural stuff manifest there! Ok I wasn't in a great place spiritually but I had still seen tremendous manifestations of His glory hit that factory over the years. Once as I sat there with a guy who was a supervisor I just felt that wine bubble up on the inside of me. It began to overpower me and I knew that I was about to be undone right in front of the factory supervisor! I had learned not to pull back, no way, this thing had to come out. As I allowed that sweet wine to bubble up on the inside suddenly myself and the supervisor started to laugh. That laughter soon became a drunkenness and that drunkenness soon looked like the two of us rolling around on the floor hammered drunk with the whole night crew watching us! The crazy thing was that this guy said that he was an atheist and beyond converting! Mmmmm not that night! This was once

normal stuff, this happened naturally every day but that was all in the past!

Then one night right in the midst of my isolation and pain He hit me again. I was working that night at the end of a production line and had the works radio speaker perched right next to me. Suddenly the Labi Siffre song 'Something inside so strong' started to play on the radio. I started to feel warm, something was happening to me. Then that same feeling of being cocooned in a bubble of electric honey whilst being immobilised and rooted to the spot started to come over me. I was undone, tears started streaming down my face, I was a wreck, I was drunk! It was as if God Himself, the one who is never far from anyone of us, the One in whom we live and move and have our being was singing over me the words of that song! The lyrics hit me so hard and I knew it was Him singing to me:

*"The higher you build your barriers the taller I become.*
*The farther you take my rights away the faster I will run.*
*You can deny me, you can decide to turn your face away,*
*No matter cause there's,*

*Something inside so strong,*
*I know that I can make it, tho you're doing me wrong so wrong,*
*You thought that my pride was gone; oh no, something inside so strong,*
*Oh, oh oh oh oh something inside so strong.*

*The more you refuse to hear my voice the louder I will sing,*
*You hide behind walls of Jericho, your lies will come tumbling,*
*Deny my place in time, you squander wealth that's mine,*
*My light will shine so brightly, it will blind you cause there's,*

*Something inside so strong,*
*I know that I can make it, tho you're doing me wrong so wrong,*
*You thought that my pride was gone; oh no, something inside so strong,*
*Oh, oh oh oh oh something inside so strong."*[6]

6 - Siffre, L. (Something Inside) So Strong (Album: So Strong), 1987.

It was all too much, I had collided with Love yet again, I was in a pool of tears. My workmates noticed my emotion and attempted to comfort me. In reality all I wanted to do was contact Donna and explain to her as excitedly as I could that He had shown up yet again!!! The following day I found myself at the local supermarket, I suddenly noticed that I was the only person in the aisle. There I was on my own yet again stood right next to the supermarket speaker. Then that same Labi Siffre song started playing again! There He was again reaching into my loneliness, revealing Love to me and showing me that we have always been One! No escaping him! I stood there yet again rooted to the spot weeping like a baby as He sang over me with words of intense unconditional Love! I had built walls of Jericho around myself but they were coming tumbling down. His love for me was so strong!

There was a knock at the door. This would prove to be the last knock ever from my gypsy brothers, "Brother David would you like to come and walk the fields with us on this fine night? The good Lord is with us as is the weather!" Although I was present physically that night, mentally I was a million miles away. I was awakening again to that reality, I felt close, not that I was ever far away! At about 4am on the darkest of nights as my dog coursed a hare through the beautiful Cotswold fields I suddenly felt His presence one more time. It may sound repetitive and I wish that I could word these moments with more variety, but it seemed to manifest just like all the other times! The way my body reacted to these incidents was the same every time. This time yet again I was cocooned in a bubble of liquid honey, my feet were rooted to the spot, I was paralysed by glory and tears streamed down my face. What does that feel like? Well in those moments you engage another realm, another world. That realm, that reality, becomes more real to you than anything around you. Time stands still and what you are experiencing

spiritually is all that matters. As He hit me again that night my dog suddenly seemed miles away, the scenery vanished from before me and I felt all on my own and saturated by Divine grace. I then heard His voice. It sounded audible but in no way was that relevant, all that mattered was the encounter and the message that He brought, "Son don't you think that I have more for you than this?" Then I heard it a second time and then a third, "Son don't you think that I have more for you than this?" There was nothing wrong with what I was doing, I knew that He wanted me to engage and enjoy my life, but He was right, there was something missing! That relationship was missing, I had replaced that intimacy with Him with other things, secondary pursuits. That night I was undone. I knew that He was revealing reality to me as He had so many times in my past. This was Love, unconditional Love, I was running with both the hare and the hounds yet He still chose to reveal Himself to me! My gypsy brothers looked at me, I know that they also felt that liquid honey, "Brother David are you ok Brother David?" My answer was an emphatic, "Yes I have never felt better." The next day I gave my 'dags' away and wondered to myself what would happen next!

# Chapter Six

## HE USES FOOLISH THINGS

People ask me all the time, "Dave how have you walked in so much glory? What are the keys? What can I do to see this stuff break out in my life?" People always look to a formula as a means of an aid don't they! I guess that the desire to engage in the supernatural and walk in identity is a noble desire though, I understand that. I suppose if I could offer any thoughts which may help or, which I believe, which may have at least helped me, then I would say that after waking up to the power of 'desire,' the second most amazing element that I have seen affect my life would be that of 'honour.' To honour another, to see value and worth in someone and in what they are carrying is an amazing way of attracting that same blessing into your life. What I value in another is ultimately what I know is priceless in my own life. Recognising someone else's virtue is ultimately me realising that the same virtue is dormant within my life and it's time for that virtue to be unearthed! I've always been more of an optimist than a pessimist, I believe that being a cynic blocks so much potential reality from breaking out in your life. Cynicism blocks

the blessing and stops human progression. I've always chosen to see value in others and have chosen to honour others even when I haven't fully understood everything they are walking in! I've chosen the path of honour as opposed to cynicism. I have spent days and weeks and months honouring guys whom I barely know. Some were people that I had only heard rumours about and caught whispered tales of their so called exploits. I never questioned the validity of the stories, I would just allow those tales to stimulate desire within me to see that same stuff break out in my life. I would spend months thinking about what I had heard, and a million times a day I would whisper silently to myself, "I honour the life of this person, I honour that realm which they are walking in. Let that same manifestation break out in my life. I honour that man." It may seem strange to you but it works! Jesus Himself knew this truth as he taught the people saying:

*"He who receives a prophet in the name of a prophet shall receive a prophets reward. And he who receives a righteous man in the name of a righteous man shall receive a righteous man's reward!"* [7]

There is a great reward that manifests as we honour what others are experiencing! As I have already mentioned sometimes I would just hear the whisper of a story and I would allow the possibility of that being a truth to connect with me. I remember hearing once that there was a man by the name of John Scotland who got so incapacitated by God that he was in a continual drunk state for 7 years straight! That's all that I heard. I had never met John, I had never heard him preach, I never saw a picture of him and I knew nothing about him at all! Yet for an entire year off the back of a silently whispered tale I uttered the words, "I honour John Scotland. I honour that realm of wine and reality that he walks in. I honour the intoxication that he walks in and the glory that he carries. I want that same intoxication to

7 - Matthew 10:41 (King James 2000 Bible).

break out in my life!" A year later I was invited to Holland and walked into a meeting and a friend said to me, "Dave there's someone that I want you to meet, he's a great guy and I know he'd love you, his name is John Scotland!" The moment that my eyes met Johns I fell to the floor. John grabbed my foot and for 10 minutes he shook me with that same glory that I had honoured in secret for an entire year previously! Honour had done it's perfect work! Another time I heard mention of a guy by the name of Jason Westerfield. Someone shared with me a little of Jason's crazy supernatural exploits and instantly I knew I wanted to connect with him. For a year I honoured him in my heart, I never heard him preach, never saw a picture of him and never met him but I honoured his life and ministry in secret. It wasn't long before I started to make a connection with Jason and for the Divine to tell Jason that he needed to cancel his hotel room and come to stay with me and my family in our home! The very rooms where I had honoured this guy in secret were the same rooms where we eventually sat down together and encountered the spirit realm in! Honour, what a beautiful key and precious door to walk through to connect with the desires of your heart!

"Here watch this. This guy is a crazy man in the spirit!" A video tape was thrust into my hands and my friend left. I was ready to move forward, like never before my desire was strong to walk in and explore my connection with the Divine. That evening I watched the video tape, it was crazy. It was an interview and some footage from Indonesia featuring a guy by the name of Darrel Stott. The guy seemed like a right loon and was 'sorta' frightening in a fun way. Darrel had apparently got hit at the 'Toronto Renewal' years before and had shook so violently under the power of the Spirit for 3 months that several times he shook the screws out of his spectacles and lost his lenses! He had moved his ministry to Indonesia and apparently was seeing some crazy manifestations of God in the nation. He was a funny

looking guy, who looked a lot like an old teddy boy with sticky out ears. Apparently his Grandma would read William Branham books over him when he was a boy and would 'encourage' him with the words, "Darrel you are an ugly child but there's something about you that heaven loves!" Darrel was a wild man in the Spirit and his ministry looked like something crazy enough for me to connect with. I was done with the unreality of church life, there was no going back to that stuff, but I was so desiring a reality where heaven manifested and lives were transformed. This guy was weird, he would stagger around the stage under a heavy weight of glory three sheets to the wind, with his spectacles perched on the end of his nose and his eyes bloodshot red all the while shouting out, "Walla walla wamba, woomballa woomba, yar yar yar!" There was definitely no strict adhering to ministry protocol in anything that he did, yet there was a definite sense of heaven in the room as guys rolled around on the floor laughing hysterically!

The interview on the tape with Darrel was interesting to say the least. Darrel was sharing how powerfully the glory was manifesting in Indonesia and how the nation was in the grip of a powerful revival. Jesus was apparently appearing to Muslims in the nation and it seemed that Indonesia had gone from 5 percent Christian to over 30 percent in just 10 years! He talked about how the angels and the cloud of glory were manifesting in his life and meetings and shared how outrageous the subsequent fruit was. He shared to the camera that one day whilst in a cab in Indonesia that the cloud of God's glory started to manifest. He said that as he got out of the cab the physical cloud of glory followed him into his hotel and then into the elevator! Apparently the cloud then followed him to his room and hovered there for a while. Darrel said that as he watched the cloud suddenly angels appeared as lightnings out of the cloud and whizzed around his room! They then appeared on the wall as random shapes, the shapes of islands in the nation of

Indonesia! Darrel quickly drew down the shapes that appeared to him and the following day handed the paper to his Indonesian administrator. Harry his administrator instantly recognised the shapes on the paper as islands in the nation and hurriedly set up a 3 month itinerary for Darrel based around the shapes drawn on the paper! This was another level of glory! This tape got my attention and I booked my plane ticket to join up with Darrel for 15 days in Jakarta!

Darrel was drunk! To meet him was an experience in itself. Here I was in Indonesia with a guy who I had never met as a result of watching a dodgy XXX rated spiritual porn movie! It was 8am in the morning, I was fully jet lagged and was ready for a hotel breakfast and stiff coffee. I noticed Darrel sat in the breakfast area on his own with his head rested on the table. I joined him half wondering what he was doing. As I sat down opposite Darrel he lifted up his head and with bloodshot red eyes he slurred at me, "So we don't have meetings booked for today do we! We will see, you watch what happens today!" Within seconds Darrel's administrator showed up and said, "Darrel they all know you are here, there were no meetings planned for today but now you have two meetings this morning!"

Those meetings blew up and were typical of the entire 15 day stay. Basically we would show up at each meeting already wasted in the glory, as we would walk into the hall the worship would already be in full swing and there would be an intensity of atmosphere present which you could literally chop in half with a sword! Man it was thick with heaven, every place, every meeting was rammed with the cloud of His presence. As Darrel would start to communicate the glory would steadily and noticeably increase to the extent that within minutes Darrel would be slurring his words and his translator would be keeled over in fits of laughter. The angels of God would then begin to manifest in the room and start pulling people around! Guys would begin

to noticeably be shaken as they laughed hysterically! Often people on the floor would start to roll back and forth all over the church floor. This would start slowly as if they were being rocked gently but before you knew it they were literally being launched supernaturally and thrown all over the room. It was crazy to watch as the gatherings turned into drunken free for alls! I loved it all!

Something crazily supernatural was taking place in the nation and Darrel was obviously being honoured as a father in the whole situation. Pastors in the nation were more than just pastors, they were fathers, apostles of love, fully secure in who they were and highly respected by their congregations. Respect and honour created room for great fruit. Huge building projects were the norm in the nation. Pastors were building stadiums to hold tens of thousands of new converts and by the time the stadiums were ready they needed even bigger stadiums to facilitate all the new converts. 'Papa Darrel' was highly honoured and invited to share at all of these huge stadiums. As we visited one place I will always remember the glory that I encountered there. As Darrel preached you could tangibly feel a shift in the atmosphere of the room, Darrel then shouted out, "An angel of God has just hit that section!" As I looked towards the area that Darrel had mentioned what I saw can only be described as drunken chaos. In one section of the stadium right besides me was what looked like a perfectly structured 'crop circle' manufactured via hundreds of drunken Indonesian bodies. It was as if a huge angel had dropped into the centre of that section with so much glory that it caused a 1,000 body crop circle to be perfectly created all around it! It looked like a mangled up montage of drunken limbs all connected and weaved together into a perfect circle of life! Straight away I thought, "Man I haven't come all this way for a jolly, I want to experience THAT!" I ran as hard as I could and attempted to jump right into the centre of the intoxicated wreckage! As I jumped it was as if I hit an invisible wall of

glory and I found myself being thrown backwards at a rate of knots! CRAZY STUFF.

A thought! The western church works so hard in an honest, all be it misguided, attempt to make things happen! We have programs, events, schools, conferences, outreaches, structures, formulas, meetings, pre-meeting meetings and post-meeting meetings! Man I get tired just thinking about it! And for what? All of our efforts have produced what? Think about it, apart from more conditioned thinking and a deeper dependency upon the system, what have we seen breakout as a direct result of carrying such a heavy workload? What I saw breaking out in Indonesia seemed so effortless! It was obvious being there that He was building His church and it was obvious that this was the fruit of his labours and not ours. It was all Gods fault!

This truth was beautifully articulated to me by a precious 24 year old pastor of a congregation of 2,500, most of whom were university students! Every Sunday Pastor Jonathan holds 5 services, it was incredible to watch. 500 would come in and 500 would go out, then another 500 would come in and another 500 would go out! The first service was at 6.30 am! In between services we would go back to Jonathan's office and wait for the next 500 guys to show up. It didn't take long for me to feel humbled and slightly overwhelmed. I was so impressed by what I was seeing that I felt compelled to ask Jonathan about his journey. The Pastor shared with us a little of his incredible story by saying, "One year ago I had a congregation of just 197 people! I tried all within my power to get my church to grow but nothing. It actually seemed that the harder that I worked the less the church would grow. I then had one encounter with the Divine and in one year our congregation grew from 197 to 2,500! I now realise that the harder that I work the less the church grows but the more that I rest and enjoy life the quicker

and the more exponentially the church grows! I now have a vision for a church of one million people, all students!"

This story wrecked me. In one sense it was difficult to conceive, my western mind had no grid for this 'rest' or for the enormity of the figures being thrown around. Yet here was the reality of the story breaking out all around me. Jonathan just glowed, he radiated the glory, he carried so much rest and that rest worked for him in building his congregation! This seemed foolish to me, a totally supernatural dynamic, a dynamic which western church leaders know nothing about! As we sat in those meetings and watched the glory move powerfully amongst the people I watched as the young children danced and partied with the angels. Their faces glowed as they interacted with the heavenly beings, one young girl came over to me and said, "Pastor please can you tell me how to get the angels to leave? We know how to get them to come but please tell me, how do you get them to leave?" She literally had a bright light coming from her as she laughed and begged me to give her a key which would stop the angels from playing with her and from bothering her as she attempted to take care of her school work!

I knew that in just a few days I would be leaving for home. I was full, I had received so much and had learned valuable lessons about the glory of rest and reality. There was just one more church to visit, they called it the 'angel church.' I had heard guys talking about this place, they told me that it was wild, that *millions* of angels were there and that these angels liked to play! As the locals collected us from the hotel foyer I got talking with them. It was obvious that these guys were from the church congregation, they were lit up and were hammered drunk in the Holy Ghost! As I talked with them I asked them about the claims of "Millions of angels being at their church", "Oh yes there are," said one guy, another then said to me, "They are all different sizes, some are huge, others smaller, some are

small enough to put in your pocket! Oh, and they love to play!" Mmmm, a mobile angel, I like that! I told them that I just wanted it and was up for it all! What I experienced that night is hard to explain and was even harder to process at the time! Our western mentality so loves a plausible, palatable, understandable gospel! Yet our western, charismatic church is so void of power and life even though it feels that it can explain everything! As I walked into the hall that night I noticed that something was missing, There were no chairs at all in the room! No chairs, just a wide open space. Then I noticed that the deacons weren't stood there wearing suits, handing out hymnals and wearing name badges! Hell no, these guys were stood near the walls of the hall and they weren't packing Bibles but were loaded with huge sofa cushions! Then I noticed that guys were rolling across the floor of the building at a supersonic rate of knots! It was crazy and impossible to do without some sort of physical help. Yet there was no-one pushing them! They were just rolling, rolling very quickly! I then discovered why the cushions were necessary, as guys hurtled along and were about to hit the walls of the hall one of the deacons would then drop to one knee and use the cushion as a buffer to soften their impact!

This thing was nuts but as I said I was up for it. That night as I danced by myself in the glory I suddenly felt someone take a-hold of my hands. My eyes were closed so I had no idea who it was, I just went with it. As I continued to dance suddenly the glory started increasing on me and eventually I found myself laid out on the floor. As I lay there I felt myself being rocked back and forth, then before I knew it I found myself being launched around the room! For 3 hours the angels rolled me around the hall as I laughed like a little child. It was crazy. As I went back ↻ the hotel that night absolutely hammered drunk and totally ⁀nfused someone showed me a load of pictures they had taken ⁀e whilst I was on the floor. To my surprise on every single ⁀e there were orb like lights all over my body! The angels

had actually shown up on the pictures as balls of light, as weird looking worlds of light. What a stupidly crazy night! Now for you cynics out there who find great pleasure in tearing apart encounters and experiences that don't fit within our theological remit and who will always ask, "Well what was the point of that and what is the lasting fruit?" Can I just suggest this, that night my life was radically and eternally transformed, I was supernaturally liberated from so much religious bullshit which had built up over the years and I have never ever looked back! I encountered a realm that night which marked me forever and which opened me up to an angelic reality which I still walk in to this day! Added to that, the church where these things were taking place now operates an international ministry and plants new churches all over the world seeing tremendous, continual fruit! Not too foolish hey!

# Chapter Seven

## MOMENTUM IS A GREAT THING

It was pretty obvious to me that Darrel had tapped into a realm of reality which my heart had always yearned for. It was slowly beginning to manifest for me, freedom was starting to take over my life. That trip to Indonesia changed me forever and I so desired to be around that anointing some more. I heard that Darrel was in Europe so I decided to trek with him on his travels. I took my boy Josh with me over to Northern Ireland and connected with Darrel whilst he was in Bangor which is known as '*The Valley of Angels*!' This whole trip was a blur! In one meeting the whole congregation got lit up as Darrel attempted to slur his way through yet another sermon. In all ~ness Darrel's preaching was not the greatest, his theology not ~ound, BUT in every service at some point you would sense ~osphere shifting in the room and stuff would pop! This ~we all showed up, it certainly wasn't about Darrel's ~ ability to layer deep and instructive theology, hell ~ll about the encounter, about feeling alive and ~e.

I felt something of a connection with him and I contacted the administrator of the trip asking if there was still room for this guy to come with us. I was told that all the slots were filled but I just knew he would join us. The next day someone dropped out and my friend Ern (he has asked to not be named in this book so for this books purposes he will be known as 'Ern'), signed up to join us! Myself and Ern were asked to go with a man who would host us to his home. We were told that he had a motor home in his garden where we would sleep, man it sounded great and I had visions of a Led Zeppelin tour bus type situation all rigged out with cable television and mini bars. Alas as we arrived we were shown to a rusty old two berth caravan which only had one bed in it and what appeared to be a soiled and moist quilt laid over it. Welcome to the glamorous life of a missionary!

Those meetings were '*Darrel meetings*;' Darrel's meetings blow up, so as expected these gatherings were pretty much off the chain. Cancers dissolved, limbs were healed, the prophetic words given were powerful and as usual the glory was freakish. As a team we were continually wasted, this was the high of the Most High, there were no drugs involved just random trips being given out by 'The Pusher.' One of the meetings was particularly drunk, Ern and I showed up pretty late as we had got hit somewhere and glued to a subway wall for an hour or so. There was a ramp which you needed to walk up outside the building to get into the hall and I will always remember that night because as we walked up the ramp we suddenly found ourselves having to walk through a physical wall of glory. It was crazy, at the front of the ramp you would feel nothing, then half way up the ramp you actually felt yourself walking into a cloud of intense presence!

We were stunned. As we entered the back of the hall we were greeted by a rather unpleasant Darrel who was bemused by why we were so late showing up. After explaining our dilemma to

him he asked us to go and stand behind a certain lady near the front of the meeting, "Look, the angels are all around that girl, go down there and stand near her, Woomballa Wommba!" We couldn't see any angels but we obeyed and stood right behind the girl as the worship continued. As we stood there suddenly the girl shook, it was pretty violent and also pretty obvious that she had just involuntarily been targeted from above. An incoming bliss bomb had nailed her and it was all God's fault! As the girl shook Ern and I both watched as a physical fountain of gold plumed out of her back and scattered all over the floor around us! It looked like a plume of golden glitter, it fell everywhere, all around us! In those moments your natural mind cannot comprehend what you have witnessed, we both started looking at each other and reasoning whether maybe the lady's cardigan had started to disintegrate in some weird way. This seemed way more plausible for us to deal with than to comprehend that a physical fountain of gold had shot out of the lady's back! My wife Donna experienced this phenomena once herself as she shopped for clothes, as she stood by a certain rail a plume of gold fountained into the air. Not that she needed a sign from heaven to shop - Donna took this as an indication that the Divine wanted her to spend, spend, spend! We've seen so many manifestations of this nature, gold dust falling, gemstones falling, feathers falling, as a matter of fact as I've been writing this book I've had feathers materialising above me and falling on me! People get so angry about this stuff, "What's the point of that? What fruit has come from it?" My question is this, "Why does there always have to be an explanation and resulting fruit from these manifestation? Why can't God be God and why can't we just enjoy a supernatural ride?" I choose to honour the supernatural, with or without resulting fruit!

Those few days in Denmark were totally supernatural. We saw many healing's including the instant healing of our hosts hands who had always suffered with a crazy rash type deal. He asked

me for prayer, his hands were covered in cracks and sores, it was pretty nasty and looked awfully painful. I just cursed the symptom and commanded healing to flow. As we walked into the house the following morning for breakfast the guy looked pretty pleased to see us and was sat there with totally normal hands and fingers, he was healed and his hands looked as good as new. Ern and I knew that we were there for way more than a few meetings. There was something going on with us which was so powerful and was obviously one of those Divine set ups!

As we would go back to our little caravan each night to rest and would curl up top to toe under that moist and smelly quilt the glory of God would roll over that caravan in waves. Wave after wave rolled through that place. We would physically feel the wave rolling in and at times would start screaming and laughing as the whack would hit us again and again and again. This was no coincidence, this was a God incidence, we had been set up and put together in an amazing way! We had little sleep, 4am one night, 6am another night, too drunk to sleep, too excited to drift off. As we laid there in that rusty caravan our conversations turned to revival. Our journeys were so similar, both of us had yearned for a revival that was out of control, both of us loved the glory and wanted to be carriers of life and both of us had walked through major disappointments due to pain and hurt we experienced in church situations.

Over those few nights we shared our deepest desires with each other, our stories of encounters, of dreams and visions. We were on the same page with so much, all we wanted to see was a wildfire break out of heaven on earth which carried with it ramifications of epic proportions. Where could you go in the UK to experience His glory? Where were the hot spots? Who were the guys who carried the anointing and who was making room for freedom to manifest? So many times we had both been ejected from tame meetings as we began to laugh or manifest

something spiritual and we had both come to the conclusion that the UK was spiritually as dry as a ships biscuit and harder than a coffin nail! We also came to the conclusion that when we returned to Wales that we would do all that we could to pray until something changed. Over those few days we made a covenant with each other, we vowed to seek God until something new broke out in our lives and in the lives of those within the UK.

# Chapter Eight

## TO SEE A WILDFIRE REVIVAL

*"What I saw taking place were some major fires hitting Wales, but the fire that I saw I could only describe as wildfire. It is fire that will explode and a fire that is dangerous. It is fire that cannot be domesticated (we will not be able to say, 'I will take some of that fire, put in in a hearth and it will keep me warm' - no this is wild fire.) And I saw that the wild fire began to jump across the border, because what is in England currently can be domesticated and it will be domesticated and will be tamed and will be controlled, in fact it will come to where some will say, 'this really is under our jurisdiction.' And what it is waiting for is for the fire that is wild to come and to impact that. In other words England needs a Welsh revival. Not only England, for since 1991 I have been saying when it hits this whole thrust of the Spirit is in order that Europe might be saturated. This is Europe's day and it is a long day- because at the end of the day it is the Islamic world that God is targeting.*

*But it will not take place without a Welsh revival.*

*England needs a Welsh revival, England needs a Welsh revival. I hear a call going out saying, 'We must have a Welsh revival!' People standing*

*in England saying, 'We must have a Welsh revival. We must have the wildfire.' We must have it, where is it going to come from? It is going to come out of Wales. In other words God does not want to give a revival in Wales, he wants to give a Welsh revival. That is why you cannot import revival into Wales- you can import many things but you cannot import a Welsh revival. It will have all the characteristics of wildfire, you cannot begin to control this!"*

Martin Scott declared this word over Wales in March of 1999. This word became our fuel for what was about to follow. For nine months Ern and I set our faces to seek the Lord. Our minds were fixed, we were going after an explosion of reality and nothing would stand in our way. No-one really understood this commitment, it was strange to most and could easily have been misinterpreted as we separated ourselves from church life and from cynical people. It seemed important that we were focused, we both felt something of a weight of responsibility to pray this thing through. In no way did this feel like a burden to us, as a matter of fact we were excited about our venture and felt strongly empowered by grace to see it through. Initially it all seemed a bit strange, I mean we barely knew each other and here we were spending hours together each day pacing back and forth declaring a shift for the nation of Wales. We were still both working at the time, I was running my own pest control business and I was also working full time as a Youth Worker at a Christian cafe. Even though we both lived pretty busy lives our commitment to be with each other and to pray was unwavering. We were focused and we did all that we could to meet together each evening and to spend days together on the weekends.

Looking back it all seems a bit crazy, I mean when things eventually started to break out it looked a lot like what we had already experienced in our 2 Berth *'love shack'* in Denmark! Wave after wave of heavy drunken intoxication washing over our lives, a knowing of an ever present union with God Herself!

Yet there always seems to be a battle to experience this bliss, it's as if mankind feels that unless it battles through and arrives at a sense that we have *done* something to see it break out then somehow it can't be a legitimate reality. It's obvious to me now 10 years down the road, after many shifts in my thinking and much time spent pondering my years of stupidly misguided devotions that actually I was never far from Him! We were always One, the only separation that existed was the separation within my thinking! There was a gap in my thinking which needed to be bridged, the thought that to experience God I needed to draw close and show Him that I was desperately wanting some sort of encounter or lifestyle of intimacy. In reality I was the one who placed the hoops there, I felt (or the religious frameworks in my thinking felt) the need to have to pursue a God who in reality is closer to us all than the very air that we breath. Something inside my thinking thought that a *process* was necessary in order to walk in reality, this was far from the truth! Once we realise these precious truths we save ourselves so much time and mental torture, the torture of not knowing whether He will or won't respond! Once we recognise that He's near, always was and always will be, and that we are continually connected to His reality then it makes things a whole lot easier!

It's easy looking back to see where maybe we were misguided in some areas. So many *after the event* can give a professional discourse on where you went wrong and how it could have been so much easier! Yet in reality we always start off with what we know, we work with whatever is manifesting in our religious frameworks and we go along with whatever desire is manifesting in our lives. Our desire was to see a Wildfire Revival, our minds told us that to see this break out we needed to give ourselves to some sort of holy devotion in prayer. So we did! Day after day of contending, of pressing, of seeking, of shaking our fists at a God who was always very present! Hours would pass by as we encouraged each other in our quest for reality. Together we would

that to be fulfilled that we need to see certain manifestations? I mean if I walk in Bentley's anointing I won't be walking in Wigglesworth's anointing and if I see what Wigglesworth saw break out in my life then I still wont be seeing what Branham saw, and if I see what Branham saw I still won't be seeing what Enoch saw! I mean when does it all end!!!!" For me the end had come, I had reached home, no more striving, no more contending, life had come!

It was 2005 and Todd Bentley was holding some gatherings in Wales around that time and I signed up to go. It was a crazy conference for me personally; it was also the tour where Todd had his first meltdown and had to take 18 months out of ministry to recover. While I was at that conference I knew that things were about to massively shift for Donna and I. The Holy Ghost spoke with me that I was to leave my secular work and start trusting Him for money. This was a real stretch. Donna and I had always struggled financially and this was the first time in my life that I felt we were doing ok for money. I said to God, "If you want me to give up my work then confirm it in this meeting by asking someone to give me a gift of £1,000." At the end of that gathering a guy came over to me and pushed an envelope into my hands with the words, "Here I should've given you this a week ago but was disobedient and held onto it!" As I opened the envelope there inside was a cheque for £1,000 exactly.

While I was there at the conference I stayed at a B&B in the nights. On the last night there I woke up at 3am to what I can only explain as, 'I was in the womb of God itself!' It was crazy. I felt that I woke up inside the very womb of the Divine. It was as if I was in a pulsating womb of intense love and life and I was about to be birthed out in some incredible way. I was in some crazy spiritual incubator. The walls of the room seemed to be pushing in and out as the Divine breathed away and all along I

was in this intensely charged womb of Divine Life. I knew that something crazily drunk was taking place here!

Ern and I were nearing the end of a crazy 9 month season of our lives. Looking back so much of that journey now seems strange and unnecessary yet at the time it was all we knew and was maybe right for where we were at! After 9 months of crazy prayer one night we were at Ern's home, it had been another night of strange intercession stuff and we were just having some tea before I left for home. Suddenly from the corner of the room a roaring sound started to manifest, it was loud, almost audible and it instantly got both of our attentions. Then a wave of glory rolled over that room which left both Ern and I screaming because of it's intensity! It seemed to take a minute or so to roll through and all the while we just knelt on the floor screaming like frightened kids. As it subsided Ern looked at me and said, "What was that?" I just replied as I took my spectacles off and said, "That was God dude, I've waited all my life for this, I'm not going anywhere!" Then another wave hit and then another and suddenly we were both caught up into a realm of heavenly glory which is pretty much indescribable. Colours, sounds, sights, voices, people! Ern said that he heard voices like excited children saying, "They're starting to believe, they're coming up here, this is so exciting, they have no idea what is waiting for them!" All the while I just had my head buried into the floor seeing vision after vision of heavenly reality. After 3 hours of being together overwhelmed and overcome by the spirit realm I left Ern's home knowing that nothing would ever be the same again!

As I woke up the next day I realised that something was different. I don't know there just seems that there are moments in life where reality is fully appreciated and fully lived. As I drove to Abergavenny that day to work at the little cafe that I managed I realised that I was fully clothed in glory. There

was an intensity of 'presence' on me which was new, it was heavy and it didn't feel like it was going away. I knew that it was strong and that if others got around me that they too would feel it. I had heard stories from church history where guys like Charles Finney carried such a weight of glory that he would walk into shops or places of work and suddenly guys would begin to be convicted of their loose living as a direct result of the presence on Finney's life. Over the years I have yearned to carry this presence, to walk in such a realm of glory that others would feel and experience heaven in their midst. I once chatted with a guy who was friends with the late Lonnie Frisbee. Lonnie was a crazy man of God who was instrumental in moves of God in California in the early 70's. I asked my friend what it was like to be around Lonnie, he just looked at me and said, "Dave when you were with Lonnie you weren't with a person but were with a presence! When Lonnie walked in the room you were suddenly aware of God!" I always wondered what that would be like? To walk into a shop like Smith Wigglesworth and have guys suddenly start to weep because of the presence that you carried?

That day I felt something different on my life. I needed that morning to go into a book shop on the way to work, as I walked into the shop and stood there waiting to be served suddenly a lady came over to me and started weeping! It was as if as soon as she got near to me she was impacted by the same presence which I was still feeling from the night before! She held onto my hand and with tears streaming down her face said to me, "I want what you've got!" At that moment a second lady came over to me and with tears streaming down her face and her makeup running down her cheeks she said to me, "I want what you've got, I want what you've got!" Unbeknown to me at that very moment a lady who was walking past the shop suddenly got rooted to the spot as if she was being hypnotised by some strange force! She instantly felt compelled to drop her plans and to walk into that

little book shop! Suddenly I had a third lady grabbing a-hold of me, who with tears streaming down her face said, "I want what you've got!" This was different, yes I'd personally experienced stuff before but never to the extent where others around me got impacted in such a way! I just shared with these 3 ladies, "Last night I was in the throne room of heaven, I encountered God in an amazing way, what you are feeling right now is His Divine presence and Love!"

As I left that place I realised that I was late to get to a little prayer meeting that I ran each Tuesday. On the way to the meeting I heard the words, "Give a portion to 7 and also to 8!" Weird, but it seemed real. As I got into the room there were 7 guys there waiting for me! As I sat there and began to explain what had just take place with me in the book shop that same anointing instantly started to touch the 7 guys with me. One by one they started to weep and one by one each said, "I want what you've got!" Suddenly I had 7 guys with tears streaming down their faces holding on to me all being impacted by that crazy and very tangible Divine reality. Then the door opened and an 8th guy walked in who said to me, "I want what you've got!" I then remembered the phrase that I heard, "Give a portion to 7 and also to 8!" This guy was the 8th and he also got hit! My phone started to ring. It was Ern, "What's going on there?" He asked. Before I could answer he spurted out, "I'm hiding in the cleaning cupboard in work! The glory is so strong, so heavy that I couldn't stop laughing and I knew that I needed to get away from people, so I hid in the cleaners cupboard!" This was different! Could this be the Wildfire that Martin Scott had prophesied 7 years previous which would come out of Wales? Whatever it was I knew that this thing had the potential to transform many lives. That day I gave up my job at the cafe and readied myself for whatever was about to hit next!

believe will be the next great thing! Invariably this often leads guys to disconnecting from real life and pulling away from the greatness of opportunities all around them, BUT they so feel that the *Lord* is on this thing so hey leave them to it. Soon reality hits home when after years of brown nosing their way to mediocre success and smashing down ever possible doorway into a preaching opportunity they suddenly find themselves *on the road* doing their first ever ministry tour! Woop woop. All visions of grandeur soon drop away from sight as they find themselves sleeping on cold floors, speaking at venues holding only 15 warm bodies and collecting offering baskets littered with blank offering sheets, empty Starbucks cards and more bubblegum wrappers and loose shrapnel than you can shake a stick at! I never *built* a ministry, if anything I had a ministry built around me by guys who recognised the glory I was carrying and who took time to arrange ministry stuff around my life. My theology wasn't great, as a matter of fact my thoughts on so much stuff were absolutely screwed, but there was a glory manifesting on me and in my home which was tangible. I realised, as did others, that it was this glory which would make the difference and not the correctness of my preaching!

We were seeing so much stuff manifest. Wherever we went the glory would just break out. Our homes were becoming hubs of angelic activity and crazy supernatural events. Our kids were beginning to encounter heaven as were those who came to visit us. Every day seemed like an encounter, we were no longer desiring an encounter of a lifetime but were now realising that we were living a lifestyle of encounter. Our days were continually disrupted by supernatural activity, our nights were also getting pretty crazy as wave after wave of glory rolled through. One night I remember waking up in the early hours, I remember that before my eyes opened I became aware of heaven manifesting in the room. It felt as if a million eyes were all looking in on me and that all of heavens stares were bearing down on me. It was

the craziest feeling. The only way that I could explain it would be this - imagine if in the middle of the night whilst you were fast sleep that you were transported to a huge football stadium. You were then placed right in the centre of the football pitch and left there all alone. Then the stadium was filled with 100,000 people and all the lights were switched off and you were left all alone! You then wake up and before you can open your eyes you just know that you are in a totally different place and that you are not alone! You then become aware that 200,000 eyes are all watching you in complete silence! This was exactly what this one experience felt like! It was crazy, I had no understanding to it, yes I know that it was some sort of supernatural encounter but I have no idea of why or what! Someone may say, "Well what was the point of that?" I understand! It seems foolish, the western mind can struggle with something so unusual and something so random, YET the reality is this - somehow I encountered heaven and somehow for days and weeks after I felt a great connection with that same heaven and that same heaven broke out everywhere that I went!

Ern felt that it was time to start to let others in the church know that stuff was starting to break out. One day at my home he had a vision where he saw a conference flyer with the words '*Closer to the Flame*,' written on it. A date was set for March 2006 for the conference which just so happened to be the exact day of the 7 year anniversary of Martin Scott's Wildfire prophecy. Ern's desire by hosting this conference was to inform whoever showed up that together we had started to encounter God and that for us things were now different. Martin was invited to speak as was Godfrey Birtil and Sharon Stone (the preacher and not the rather attractive blonde who maybe should have worn underwear in the film Basic Instinct!)

Ern was to host the conference with a cool guy who was recognised as a prophet in Wales at the time but the guy pulled

out and I was asked to step in and help with the hosting. The whole event was drunk! The glory was super intense. Guys showed up from all over the UK and in each session the mist of Gods presence hovered over the people. In one of the afternoon sessions I will always remember that as I attempted to share the stories of all the crazy stuff we had been seeing over the last year how loud the noise was in the room. It was chaotic, the fire of God burned through that place as we just simply shared the stories of glory breaking out wherever we went, (it was actually after these meetings and after hearing these stories that Godfrey wrote the song 'Are you ready, ready, ready!')

In one of the sessions Sharon Stone stood up and read out something of a statement, it basically endorsed the fact that something new had been born into the nation of Wales, that the Wildfire was now flowing and that whatever was happening was a legitimate move of the spirit born in Wales. Those meetings were both drunk and seriously intense. One session Martin Scott shared how now was the time for this baby to be stewarded and helped to grow. Every word exploded within us as he communicated the reality of what was breaking out around us. He finished his sermon with the words:

*"A baby has been born in the of Wales, who will look after the baby?"*

He then dropped the microphone on the floor and sat down. Ern and I both looked at each other and knew that we needed to respond. We both walked forward along with several others and expressed our willingness to see this baby called 'Wildfire' spread through the nations.

We were so drunk at that event. We weren't the only ones experiencing this glory, many stood up and shared stories of visions, dreams, encounters and even translations in the spirit. Each session blew up, at times the noise was deafening as the glory hit the people. I will always remember that last evening session, we arrived late as we were so drunk at the restaurant

that we totally forgot what the time was. As we walked in to the room Godfrey was stood there with his guitar ready to play and the place was rammed with people. I walked over to Godfrey and looked over the people and I could see a tangible mist over the heads of all sat there. Godfrey looked at me and said, "This is wild man," I knew what he meant, this was pretty intense in every way. That night blew up, the glory that manifested in the room that night was off the chain, something new and exciting was beginning to happen and there was no mistaking it's impact. Those visiting that conference would not have seen a polished performance at all! So many conferences these days are so *correct*, so mechanically operated, everything runs so smoothly, so meticulously, yet there's one missing ingredient in so many! This was raw! We would stand up hammered drunk not having a clue what to say or what we were doing! As our friend Jim Drown would say, "I'd rather be an amateur in the new than a professional in the old!" Sadly there are a lot of old 'pro's' out there! We were utter amateurs, yet amateurs who were starting to see something radically new! It was gloriously raw!

Whatever was going on in our homes was increasing, days were spent intoxicated on the sofa, weeks blissfully spent continually aware of Divine union. Most church leaders wouldn't touch us with a barge pole! We were way too controversial and unpolished to be accepted by mainstream leaders. It was the wild women in Wales who made room for us and our weirdness. Guys like Karen Lowe and Deb Chapman from Llanelli, Joanne Gravell and Sarah Trinder were the ones to embrace us and who stupidly invited us into their lives and congregations. Whilst denominations were still wrangling over the issue of whether a woman should hold an office in the church, these ladies were already proving themselves to be true apostles in the nation! Mothers, who were more interested in seeing change break out in the UK than protecting their stupid reputations. These women instantly stood with us whilst the men gathered together

and discussed their options! (They also hung around in the hard times and showed love to us, offering us priceless wisdom when everything went tits up!)

The first Sunday morning when we preached at Karen's church was so drunk. We just stood there and shared the stories of the encounters we were having and then asked guys if they wanted prayer. Pretty much everyone responded and as we laid hands on them the glory of God touched them powerfully. I will always remember one guy in particular called Nigel who just as he was about to receive prayer from us shouted out at the top of his lungs, "God I just want to get pissed!" Get pissed Nigel did as the glory of God hit him half sideways! Man that sort of stuff would instantly get shut down in most places, but that's what these gatherings were like, they were raw, real and honest!

Sarah Trinder transitioned recently into another realm of reality, I miss her so much and will always love her as a dear mother and friend. One day we decided to go and visit her at her little church office in Pontllanfraith, Wales. Sarah was and still is one big, loud and crazy woman of love, a true embodiment of life itself! Yet in all of her craziness in the spirit there was a sensitivity which she carried and a love for Wales and for revival which was incredible. As we walked into that room the glory of God just hit us all. For an hour Ern and I prophesied over Sarah as she sat there weeping in the glory. As we finished sharing and as Sarah composed herself she looked up at us and said, "I want you to come and speak to our extended leaders meeting, then I want you to come and minister at the church."

A couple of weeks later we showed up at the church for a gathering of about 25 leaders and 'almost leaders!' What happened that night was just incredible to behold. Our meetings were slightly different, there was no real structure or form to them, no we would just show up and random stuff would take place. That night I can vividly remember everyone sat around

as we started to share the stories, then a few girls started to giggle because they had looked at their hands and gold flakes had started to appear on them. I then felt that I needed to pray for one lady in particular. As I laid my hand on that lady all of a sudden a physical bolt of lightning flashed from behind her and hit her clean off her seat. Instantly it was as if some sort of strange chain reaction happened in the room and a physical wind blasted right through. As it did a great friend of mine got hit backwards off her chair, landed on her head, trapped between the wall and her seat, somehow stayed there and all you could see was her two boots waving in the air as she vibrated away! None of us had ever seen that intensity of glory, neither had we ever seen a visible bolt of lightning flash through a room before! There was a power that we were beginning to see manifest, we knew nothing of how to *make* it happen and were fully aware that it was beyond our control!

It wasn't long before guys started to invite us all over the UK. Wherever we went we would be joined by a whole bunch of guys who just wanted to be around whatever it was that was breaking out in our lives. We soon visited a home of some guys in Bristol who would ram their living room, kitchen and stairs with people every time they opened up their home for a gathering. It was normal for them to have 40 guys sitting wherever there was floor space as they hosted a meeting. One day as we arrived and started to share every one of us saw that same visible bolt of lightning shoot in through the window and out through the back of the house. The flash was so bright that even if you had your eyes closed you would still see it flash through. As you can imagine when stuff like that happens you suddenly get a shift in the atmosphere and usually a few guys get encouraged!

Lots of leaders wanted the *glory*, they just didn't want the package that it came dressed in! Lots threatened to have us in but on second thought after re-realising how strange, drunk

and totally obnoxious that it looked soon found themselves reconsidering. As Jesus said regarding John the Baptist, a wild man in the spirit, a true maverick who ate bugs and drank honey, "What did you go out to see?"[8] As with John this package was slightly different, yet it carried with it all of the hallmarks of reality! Looking back I now take my hat off to any leader who was willing to invite or support us!

One sweet pastor deliberated for a while before inviting us to his church, man the guy was so filled with fear after hearing how wild this thing truly was. We pretty much would always show up to a place with at least one car load if not two car loads of some of the strangest looking guys on the planet. I mean these guys were attempting to save this world whilst looking like they lived on another! We were always late, this was usually due to us getting so hammered drunk in some service station somewhere that we all lost not just track of time and day but also why we were even at the services in the first place! As we arrived over an hour late at this venue I will always remember the look on the pastor's face who was anxiously awaiting our arrival in the car park. As we literally rolled out of the car, (me wearing a monk's robe and ringing a bell,) his face shouted out the words, "NO not this, anything but this; this will be the end of everything I have worked so hard to build in my life!" As a matter of fact the opposite was true as the glory of God hit that place and the lightnings of God whizzed around the room, life came! That weekend the people in that place were transformed, some even had thick, sticky oil which started to run down the walls of their homes as the glory touched them in a new way. Incredible!

We were way past the point of caring how people perceived this whole thing, thankfully we had been delivered of that man pleasing, man fearing junk. We were not the ones in control of

8 - Matthew 11:7 (New International Version).

this flame, this was out of our control and we were just going along for the ride. The problem when you have to visit Scotland is that Scotland is a long 8 hour drive away, 8 hours is a long time to be in a car with a bunch of wide eyed, jacked to the max Holy Ghost junkies.

By the time we arrived into Troon we were wasted. Now I know that these days if a meeting has any joy on it that it could result in a few guys getting carried out. In our gatherings we would rock up to the gathering so hammered that usually we would need to be carried in! We were not dependent upon the gatherings for our intoxication, as a matter of fact the gatherings at times would become a hindrance to our intoxication! By now we were a good few months into this drunken glory tour of the UK and we had all picked up a few props on the way! As we staggered into that meeting in Troon all I can remember is falling about the place huffing on peoples heads! One woman's head seemed to hold particular interest for me and I just held it and snorted and snorted and snorted her hair all the while saying, "There's a lot of glory on the roots of glory!" Little did I know that this lady was the *main* prophetic voice for Scotland! Neither did I realise that she would get so offended that she would walk straight out of the meeting! Whilst all this was going on Ern staggered around with a huge foot long syringe type implement and had people sitting still in their seats so that he could pretend that he was injecting them with the Holy Ghost! Some got instantly drunk, others instantly angry and anxious! Some left, I understand why but for those who rode it out the glory of God manifested in that place in an outrageous way!

One thing that the angels taught us was that heaven was a fun place! We knew that it was time to put the fun back into fundamentalism. Half of the issue with the church in the UK was that it had lost it's humorous bone, it was way too uptight and starchy. We started rolling into places dressed as monk's and

nuns, wearing pyjamas and dressing gowns, some guys would show up dressed as doctors and would help the congregants to get over their religious ailments! It was fun!! Guys would ask us, "Why all the costumes? Why the gimmicks?" We knew that what they were really saying was, "Why does it have to be so offensive and fun? Why can't it come in a package which appeases my religious framework?" So much offence, so little time to get concerned about it!

One day we had a phone call from France, "Hello we are holding a conference in Paris, one of our speakers has cancelled, can you get here by tonight?" It was my son's birthday party but we hurriedly packed and arrived in France that night! Someone collected us that night from the airport and drove us to the gathering. We were told on the way to the meeting that another guy who had a huge international ministry would be speaking first and that we would then take the stage. As we walked into the building we were already hammered drunk! There were about 300 guys present and the 'main' guy was just wrapping up his talk. The atmosphere seemed flat but hey what's new! Suddenly the lady at the front says, "Now our two guests from Wales will come and share with us!" We were hurried forward and the moment we started to talk our translator instantly got drunk and fell to the floor. Soon the whole front row started buckling over as the glory just started to blast guys. We had no idea of what to do so we just shouted out, "If you want this then come forward!" Half of the congregants came forward as the other half left!

We had been in the room for less than five minutes and already the place was in utter chaos! Apparently we were due to address a bunch of leaders the next day but the *main* ministry guy made sure that we were taken out of that equation as it was all too hot for him to handle! I'm pretty sure that it was while we were in France that we were accused of carrying the 'false joy!' Yep

*false joy*! It's apparently a new tool used by demon forces to oppress the body of Christ! It was all messy but for those who rode the offence and were willing to hang around for a while the fruit was glorious!

This drunkenness must have seemed so foolish to so many. For me it was the very wisdom of God and a manifestation of His divine grace into my life. We showed up in Bradford, England for two days of meetings, as usual a whole bunch of us showed up full of glory! I was due to share on the last night and by the time I got up the whole place was charged with presence. As I shared that night I will always remember how every fibre of my being felt charged and electrocuted with life. I felt as if I had been in a trance for days, heaven seemed immediately close, it was crazy but true. For two days I had staggered around the meeting hall in my monk's robe, wasted and just played with people. We had gone onto the streets in the days and I had been rolled out in a wheelchair carrying a sign which read, "Free blessings from a real monk!" I needed the wheelchair because I was so toasted in the glory - the sign was a bit of fun but it certainly drew a crowd! That day I *blessed* almost 100 people from all walks of life including our Islamic brothers! I prayed for a guy with a broken arm and his arm was totally healed. It was crazy, so much fun and had so much childlike life on it! Then on that last night as I sat on a seat and attempted to talk about our position as Sons of God there was an eerie silence that came over the room. I was so far out in the spirit that I just thought that the meeting was a complete flop! No-one was talking, no-one laughing, everyone seemed so quiet. By the end of the meeting guys were sprawled all over the floor but I just hid my head in my hands and wanted the earth to swallow me up as I thought I had just hosted the worst meeting ever! I then heard guys talking saying, "Man that was incredible, have you ever felt anything like that?" Someone then came to me and

said, "Dave that was the next level bro', that was an intensity that I have never felt before, that was the upgrade!"

This thing was spilling out everywhere. We staggered with a team of guys onto the streets of Bristol one day absolutely hammered drunk. Instantly team members started falling onto the floor and flopping around like fish right in the middle of Bristol city centre. This thing was going away! Hell no, this thing was going up front and centre, right into the heart of city centres! There's always a point where your natural mind will say, "Pull back, this is too wild, this is too crazy, pull back." We found that it was usually at the point where it was all getting crazily out of hand and you felt required to pull it in that something amazing would start to happen. Right there on the main street in Bristol as team members shook on the floor and guys staggered around hammered drunk we suddenly drew a crowd. We then stood up on benches and started preaching as the glory increased and guys felt compelled to come and inquire what on earth was taking place. In an hour we saw 30 guys right there in the midst of that drunken chaos all confess to wanting a relationship with heaven! It looked so messy, for some it was incredibly uncomfortable and cringe worthy, yet the fruit that came from it was absolutely glorious!

We arrived in Guildford, England for two days of gatherings and decided to take guys out on the streets of the town. As we settled down in the town centre we just found ourselves worshipping, banging on drums and generally making a noise and a nuisance of ourselves! I was sat in a wheelchair hammered drunk and had guys pushing me around so I could pray with the locals! It was fun but nothing much was breaking out so we decided to take a break and grab a coffee. As we sat in the coffee shop I suddenly received a call from one of our team. The guy was super excited and told us to get back to the square as soon as we could as something significant was happening. As we walked down the

hill and back into the square two things occurred to me - firstly I was beginning to sense an intense realm of glory all around the square! It was as if a square of heaven had opened up right above the area and it was somehow beaming down upon the people. Secondly I realised that about a hundred of the locals were all stood in the little square as if they had been magically drawn together by that weird presence! It was crazy and totally supernatural. By the time we got there the team were already praying for the sick and talking with the onlookers. It all seemed effortless and all seemed very kingdom like!

Soon we started to see the glory not just manifest and hit individuals but actually break out so strong that it would hit entire areas of towns. This was perfectly reflected in what took place in some village in southern Ireland where each year they would host a 'Puck Fayre.' This weird festival is held right in the centre of a village where years ago the goats of the town started bleating late at night as foreign marauders attempted to invade the area. Due to the goats diligence in waking up the locals the marauders were put to flight and now in the goats honour every year a 'goat fayre' is held. It's real strange! Basically a huge goat is put into a cage wearing a golden crown and is lofted high on a crane over the town and it remains there for 3 days whilst the locals party 24/7 in the goats honour! Then after 3 days the goat is lowered down and a marriage service is held between the goat and the young girl who is pronounced carnival queen that year! All a bit strange but hey!

We were asked to take a team to the area and to set up a tent and offer spiritual readings and dream interpretations. We arrived with a crazy team from the UK, set up our tent and by the end of the first day we were seeing so much glory manifesting and the words that we were giving people were so accurate that we were forced to put two tents up for the following day. That second day it was as if a realm of information had opened to us and we

were able to share with people details of their lives including their names, jobs and relationships. It all broke out so strong that the sons of the local fortune tellers came and threatened us to shut everything down because we were giving more accurate words than their parents and were drawing more of a crowd meaning that the fortune tellers were not getting paid their wage! We refused to take their threats seriously and carried on doing our stuff and at the end of the second day the fortune tellers themselves came to us for a reading!

At some point on that second day in Ireland a tangible realm of glory opened around the tents. You could literally walk across the street and would feel a physical wall of glory manifest. People suddenly felt a strange sense of being drawn to us and started to just walk towards the tents and stand there looking at us! They had no idea why they had been drawn, they had no idea what to say, they just stood there frozen to the spot. We would then just walk over to them hammered drunk and would start to chat with them and invariably they would get hit by reality. On the last day the glory was so thick that we found ourselves staggering through a musical procession that was taking place in the town spontaneously laying hands on unsuspecting passers by. Myself and Phil Smith just walked through the crowds laying hands on anything and anyone who moved. This wasn't a reasonable or plausible thing to do! No this was a drunk thing to do, but it worked! One after another guys got touched, one guy with a broken leg suddenly threw down his sticks and started shouting that he had been completely healed! It was nuts, so raw, so unreasonable, yet so radically right!

As we flew home from Ireland we found ourselves on the same flight as a bunch of international rugby players. These were well known stars and we were sat right in amongst them. I had a Bible open and one guy asked me what I was doing. I told him that I was 'huffing' the word of God and that I could

line him up a John 3v16! He started laughing at me as I showed him how to 'huff' the word and how the Bible encouraged us to snort 'Line upon line, precept upon precept!' He thought I was out of my mind but I quickly assured him that I wasn't out of *my* mind just out of *his* mind! He then asked what God could do? I just said that whilst in Ireland we saw gold dust coming on guys so maybe that would happen on our flight. Suddenly someone started to laugh and scream out, "Its breaking out on your face!" As we looked back up the plane we realised that gold had started to manifest all over the face of one of the burly rugby players on board and that it was his girlfriend was alerting us all to the fact! Then the guy who was sat next to me, a Welsh international rugby star started to freak out! "This is all a joke, where's the television cameras? This is candid camera isn't it? What is going on?" Nothing was going on other than heaven was breaking out on the plane. There's no escaping this glory!

We started to see the glory break out all over the place, one day it physically rained on an airplane, another time it snowed in my car! One day we walked into a pie shop in Gloucester and as we walked in the glory hit the place in the form of a tangible fire! Suddenly the guy behind the counter started to freak out saying, "It's like a fire, I'm on fire!" Myself and Phil Smith just stood there stunned as the guy turned on an industrial fan to cool himself down!

Guys from all over the world were beginning to get in touch with us, I mean this was before the days of Facebook when word travelled pretty slow and it took and age to advertise anything!

Ern and I had gone over to Atlanta to hang out with our great friend John Crowder at a conference that he was hosting. While we were there John asked us to share at an afternoon session on exactly what was going on in Wales. That session popped as we shared these simple stories, the glory was thick and it just broke out in the meeting. Somehow the recording of that meeting

ended up in the hands of a person in Scotland who proceeded in making hundreds of copies and sending them out all over the UK! We started having guys contact us from everywhere saying, "I heard that message from Atlanta, are the stories true? This sounds like an old school revival, can we meet up and hang out I want this stuff?" Guys started to travel from all over the world to be with us, we started hosting regular gatherings and inviting in guys like John Crowder and others to come and stir stuff up in the nation. Come they did and stir they did!

# Chapter Ten

## TIME FOR AN
## OLD SCHOOL SLOSHFEST

A drunk man will just do what a sober man would never consider! We've all driven through a busy city centre late at night and witnessed those who are intoxicated on liquor and who've lost all inhibition urinate merrily up the side of some building for all to see! A drunk man is just that, *DRUNK*! He doesn't care what others think of him, he's just happily doing his thing without a care in the world! I love the freedom from inhibition and crazy gay abandon that the wine of reality provides. Time after time we have staggered through busy shops or been sat in busy restaurants and suddenly you find yourself talking with someone or doing some weird random act because of this intoxication.

One time Phil Smith and I were walking through the city centre of Leeds, England absolutely blasted on this heavenly drink. Suddenly we happened upon a guy in a wheelchair who on later investigation had not been able to walk in 14 years. Being the crazy drunks that we are Phil and I decided that it

would be a great idea to ask the guy if we could pray for him. This decision wasn't inspired by faith, logic or reason, Hell no, this decision was fuelled by wine! We loosed the guy's seat belt and asked his two friends (who by the way had only ever known him as disabled,) to stand him up on his feet. As they held him there I will always remember that his legs flapped about like your granny's underwear on a washing line on a windy day. Man these things hadn't worked in a good while, it was obvious that the muscles were totally wasted away! As I got down onto my knees and placed my hands on the guys legs I was instantly filled with supernatural faith. As I commanded the guys legs to be strong we all watched as they instantly strengthened and straightened up! It was as if someone had imparted iron splints right into the guys shins! As the guy stood on his own for the first time in 14 years Phil and I encouraged him to walk back and forth. He did, and suddenly walking turned into running to the amazement of his friends and the old chap selling cigarette lighters to the side of us who instantly confessed, "I have never seen anything like this in my life!" The ecstasy on the faces of the man's friends was unreal, can you imagine what it must have been like for them? They had only ever known him as disabled and had just collected him that day for a days shopping! Anyways the wine worked, the guy ended up pushing his wheel chair away and all present confessed to wanting a relationship with the Divine!

As Phil and I walked away it all seemed a crazy blur. It was real yet somehow it all seemed  as if it was from a different world. As we both looked at each other with an expression that said, "Dude that was dope, what on earth just took place," we suddenly saw an old girl struggling to walk with the aid of a stick. We had just seen a guy get out of a wheelchair for the first time in 14 years - we felt strong in faith, this should be an easy healing after that, I mean at least this one was walking already. We walked up to the lady and asked her if she wanted healing

excitedly sharing with her about the guy in the wheel chair! "Yes I do, please pray for me," was her response! We were so stoked, I mean our faith was huge after the last healing. As we laid hands on her ready to command healing to her legs the lady quickly stopped us saying, "Before you pray I have a question, shall I take my prosthetic leg off or leave it on for the prayer?" My word!!! Instantly our faith shrank as we realised we were in way deeper than we initially thought! We just blessed her and walked on realising that she had way more faith than us!

This intoxication wasn't going away. I would spend countless days fully inebriated on this sweet presence, nothing that religion had to offer compared to this drink. Everywhere that we went it broke out, the fruit was tremendous, we were living in a revival situation and it felt amazing. I now felt that the time was right to fully honour this intoxication, it was obvious that this wasn't just some foolish sideshow, this wasn't some *bolt on* or fun side-dish when all the real stuff had finished! Hell no, this was reality, this was the way, the truth and the life in full blown manifestation.

I had started to connect a lot with John Crowder, he was a crazy man who loved this wine and was a guy who was a total abrasion and agitation to anything religious! The first time I invited John over to the UK we got into deep trouble straight away as John introduced us all to 'Toking the Ghost,' and smoking the 'Jehovah-wanna!' Pastors accused us of blasphemy of the spirit and quickly encouraged their congregants to avoid all contact with us! This was nothing new and just went to confirm to us that the UK needed to respect the party and that church leaders loved the control that they exercised over the people. Whilst John was with us he mentioned that a few years previous that he had attempted to host a 'Sloshfest' in Alaska. He shared that he thought it was a great idea but that no-one really showed up and it didn't really work out the way that he thought it may. I

knew that it was time to bring this party to the forefront in the UK, the fruit in our lives was ridiculously good and I knew that we had to share this drink with a church which seemed as dry as a ship's biscuit!

This thing was going to get drunk! I visited the home of a friend and asked him to help me to prepare a flyer for the event. This was 2007, back then social media was non-existent and advertising was a painful and usually costly experiment in attempting to draw guys to an event. We spent the day together getting the flyer ready, it was one drunken experience! Just thinking about the event, just planning it, carried with it a weight of glory that many will never experience! The flyer was ready, it was drunk, '*Sloshfest 07 - Head in the Barrel!*' Across the top of the flyer I placed a warning, 'If you have a religious spirit it will manifest at this event!' We booked a great big hall in Cardiff, Wales and everything was set! On the morning of the event I showed up absolutely toasted, we had no idea how many were going to attend, there was no way of telling how many would respond to such a crazy invitation. This was going to be either the worst decision ever or a very fortunate and heavenly inspired one! That morning as Ern and I sat there half an hour before the first session we just looked at each other realising that this could be the end of a very short lived ministry! We didn't care, we just knew that it was essential that this wine was given prominence and that the church was yet again given the opportunity to drink and live!

An hour later the hall was rammed full of people all partying hard and going crazy. To this day I still have no idea how they all found out about the event or where the majority came from! That first session as the worship came to an end I just grabbed the microphone and said, "The church is full of religious junk, we need a Holy Ghost enema, we need flushing out! If you are here

today and you know that you are clogged up with religious shit then come forward and receive your cleansing!" Two thirds of the guys present came forward and lined up! Then they all bent over and assumed a position that mimicked the insertion of the enema tube as they laughed uncontrollably and each one enjoyed their first holy enema cleanse! This whole event was drunk, this wasn't a conference, this was a joining in with the eternal celebration. Heaven isn't a library, conference or theological seminary, hell no heaven is a party, an eternal celebration of perfection and life and that's what Sloshie represented!

On the second day of the event I strapped an electronic fart machine under a random chair in the audience! As the speaker shared in the first session I would wait until there was a quiet moment and I would press the button on the handset and set the machine off under the unfortunate guys chair who had inadvertently sat there! At one point I looked back and saw the old lady sat next to this fella laughing so hard that tears were streaming down her face! I know, I'm a naughty boy but hey! Wave after wave of glory rolled through that hall, at some points the noise was deafening as guys found and experienced the liberation that comes from knowing that 'it's all gonna be OK!' We just sat there hammered, the whole event seemed to run itself. Crowder was due to share in one session and was so drunk that he hid himself from us. We looked every where for him and eventually I realised that he had squirrelled himself away into the disabled toilet! We dragged him up and made him share which looked like nothing more than him lying on the floor whilst pushing his sermon notes towards a person in the congregation who came forward and read them out to us all!

The party on the last night was extreme! Somehow in the corner of the room was stacked thousands of bottles of water and hundreds upon hundreds of packs of toilet paper? I'm still not sure how that happened and how they got there! Someone

then decided to start wrapping the toilet paper around all of the people whilst others decided to soak the entire congregation in the water! The result was some sort of mushy, watery, paper sludge all over the wooden block floor of the hall which resulted in the varnish starting to lift from the floor blocks! We managed to get some mops and guys proceeded in attempting to clean and dry the floor up before serious damage was done, whilst they heavily manifested a dose of the jerks! I was so drunk that I couldn't drive home whilst Sloshie was on, I ended up sleeping for 3 nights on Crowders hotel room floor all the while stinking like a junk yard dog! When it was all wrapped up we realised that this was another level. We had spent so much time hosting conferences and teaching events, it was all good but this event proved to us that heaven wasn't interested in increasing our knowledge as much as it's interested in us enjoying our freedom! For me it was obvious that there was no going back to conference life as we knew it!

2008 was extreme! It started with Winnie and Georgian Banov asking me to join them and a hundred guys in Israel for a 15 day drunken tour of the Holy Land. This was going to prove to be one of the craziest and drunkest excursions of my life. When I arrived in Israel I quickly realised that this was gonna be one drunk extravaganza! Each day two buses were hired to drive us through the the villages, towns and cities of Israel, these two buses were soon labeled the 'smoking bus' and the 'non-smoking bus'! One bus seemed rammed with absolute Holy Ghost hedonists of lunatic proportions, whilst the other bus was way more sedate and seemed to be filled more with guys who had signed up for a gentle guided tour of Jesus foot steps! The only guide for this trip was going to be by the wine of His presence and the glory of God! I was only ever 'gonna' be on the 'smoking bus,' this was the party bus, the crazy bus

where pile ups of bodies were common and where it was not out of place to see guys dripping with honey, oil or sherbet!

This trip was where I first met my great friend Benjamin Dunn who staggered onto the bus each day carrying with him a stack of bibles and a sweet drunken attitude. It was Benjamin who not only taught me but who *showed* me how to love humanity. Benjamin's heart for the poor and the broken and his ability to see all included in Christ was at the time radical and carried with it continual provocation. Benjamin was years ahead of the game, this was 2008 and here was a guy who was throwing money at round the world plane tickets so that he could hold his *'Around the world garbage dump tours'*! For me this attitude was stupidly radical. 'Ministry' for Benjamin Dunn wasn't about packed itineraries, pulpits and long sermons but was more about sitting in leper colonies and slums with orphaned kids! Ben's lifestyle got my attention and was a catalyst in shattering my ministerial frameworks. Also on that trip I got to meet Alex Sky the drunken Tsar, who seemed insanely good at sourcing coffee and ripe Jaffa oranges! These guys were drunk, it was awesome to realise that there were others out there who loved this heavenly reality.

Each day we found ourselves in crazy situations together. One day we enjoyed communion in the very ruins of a synagogue where Jesus Himself had spoken the words, "Unless you eat of my body and drink of my blood you have no part with Me!"[9] The atmosphere was so heavy as we enjoyed that moment together that I soon found myself crawling through the streets of Capernaum hammered drunk! Another day we were allowed to go into a Palestinian refugee camp near Bethlehem where we partied with the kids and served food to the families there. Man these rejects of society were so overwhelmed to see us! We visited because we wanted to serve them but they so wanted to

9 - Matthew 11:7 (New International Version).

serve us and they came out of their homes with freshly baked bread and tears streaming down their cheeks as they showed us way more love than we were able to offer them. We were the first westerners to be allowed into that situation, what a privilege it was to be with such sweet people. While we were there in Bethlehem we ate at a pizza shop in the area. This was a Muslim run establishment, the owner was real sick with terminal cancer yet they were all willing to serve us crazy Christians. As we all hung out in the restaurant suddenly the glory started to manifest and before we knew it bodies were stacked up all over the floor. It was a mess, it was out of control and it was very loud! Georgian then came up to me in the midst of all the chaos and says, "So Dave are you gonna preach the gospel to these guys? Get up and preach Dave!" Before I knew what was happening I found myself stood up and sharing what I then believed to be the gospel to all present aided by a translator! After a short 10 minute preach I then asked that if anyone wanted to experience God they should come forward and we would all pray for them. Suddenly the owner of the pizza shop and all of his staff came forward and prayed with us and a hundred guys gathered around and prayed with them! It was such an emotional time, such a privileged moment. Six months later a good friend went back and visited the shop, she was told by the owner that the day we walked into his establishment was the best day of his life and that on that day he realised who God was and that he was completely healed of cancer!

I love irony! I find it ironic that whilst we were in Bethlehem that we found a little porcelain baby Jesus which we added to our ever expanding bag of props, all used for intoxication purposes! He looked so precious with His little lily white body and puffed out rosy cheeks and He made a welcome addition to our ecstatic family! In no time at all the Baby Jesus became an international phenomena! Before we knew it guys all around the world were 'huffing' baby Jesus (miniature torsos of Jesus)

and the very strange looking Alien Jesus! It was all fun stuff and all an irritation to a religious system who liked their portrayals of Jesus to be that of a strong Redeemer, a resurrected Saviour who was no longer a babe but a full blown God/Man!

John Crowder and Benjamin Dunn brought their own brand of intoxicating fire to the party as they released their '*Toking the Ghost*' CD! This was nothing more than a fun and ecstatic celebration of all things mystical which dared to offer space for guys to explore their own brand of drunken spirituality outside of the church box. It was so obvious that we were beginning to see a sub-culture of Jesus radicals manifest all over the world who had always felt marginalised by a church who liked to have all of it's ducks lined up in a nice row. In no time at all house parties were being thrown by groups of radical ecstatics who had found the heavy front door of Evangelicalism slammed in their face because they dared to freely enjoy the eternal party. These parties were nothing more than mini-Sloshies where guys 'toked' on the baby Jesus and tranced out to Benjamin Dunn cd's! I fully understand why this would seem foolish to the established church, even now looking back it does seem like a strange time in my own personal evolution, yet at the time those crazy elements proved to be a powerful extension of grace and freedom for many right in the midst of an imperialistic system that offered no reality!

I missed my plane ride back to the UK! It was all something of a blur. I remember laying out in the hotel foyer hammered drunk as guys wheeled their suitcases passed me saying, "C'mon Dave it's time to leave we are all getting on the bus!" Man I hadn't even packed so I just shouted out, "I ain't going nowhere!" I arrived back in the UK a day late and totally lit up!

Within a few weeks of being home the Lakeland revival broke out in Florida. Todd Bentley was the focal point of this revival

and was a guy who was seeing some cool miracles in Florida so decided to extended his meetings which were aired live on God TV in the UK. The revival was causing something of a stir all over the world so I decided to go and check out what all the fuss was about. The hit that I took in Israel was strong, I had now been fully incapacitated in the glory for a full three months! I was in Lakeland for about 10 days and spent most of the time sharing a hotel room with my good buddy Jim Samuelson and his mate Frank who was the son of Lester Sumrall!

It was a crazy time! The meetings were ok, there was a definite sense that something was taking place and guys seemed to be enjoying their time there. All that I knew was that I was in my own personal bubble of wine which didn't seem to be abating! I wasn't there long before guys started to realise that whatever it was that I was carrying was somewhat different! In the day meetings I would be asked by the preachers of the meetings to go forward and help them minister to the thousands who had showed up wanting a little bit 'more,' and at night the guys from Todd's team would hunt me out begging me to pray an impartation to them! I mean this was the ministry team of the revivalist and they would come looking for me, a wild, Welsh, drunken oddball to pray for them! They obviously could see and feel something different resting on my life, I could feel it too, it just bubbled up from within me and 'sorta' covered me with a heavy and deep blanket of presence!

It seemed that whatever was going on in my life carried with it the capability to not just affect me but to also impact those around me. I remember one night after the meetings walking into a Denny's diner in Lakeland. All I know is as I walked in it was as if all of heaven followed me into that room! Before I knew it guys started to vibrate all over the restaurant, tables and chairs started to rattle, and for an hour I stood there watching heavenly chaos break out all over the place. Bodies were strewn

all over the floor, guys were crawling around the room, some were scrabbling around doing all within their means in an attempt to pull themselves back onto their chairs. The laughter and noise in that diner was incredible and I knew that somehow it was connected with the wine and presence that I carried. After an hour of chaos the chef came out of the kitchen, he walked up to me whilst looking around at the carnage and says, "I don't know what on earth is going on here but you have to leave!" I was promptly evicted!

This would prove to not be the only time that I would be evicted from an establishment in Lakeland! As I rocked up to the baseball stadium for one of the night meetings I will always remember how heavy the glory was on me. Man it was strong and I knew that it was touching guys all around me. Before I knew it I had a 'Fresh Fires Media Team' stood right by me with a camera and I found that a microphone was being held to my lips! I was being supported by a couple of guys on either side of me who were holding me up under an intense weight of glory as some guy started to question me about the move of the Spirit in Wales. As I attempted to answer their questions the glory got stronger and stronger to the extent that the guy interviewing me and the cameraman both got wasted and started falling around. That same glory then started to hit the guys standing all around me and soon there were bodies laid out all over the floor. Soon an usher from the revival had her hand on me and says, "I'm sorry but you will have to leave, you are causing a disturbance!" I said, "A disturbance? I thought that this was revival?" The lady looked at me and said, "This is a revival but you're causing a disturbance! You will need to be carried and placed outside the gates!" Carry me they did and they placed my drunken body right outside the gates of yet another controlled blaze! (You can actually watch that interview that I did from Lakeland

on YouTube, just put into the search bar the words 'Deceptive Welsh Wine!'[10])

What I had been experiencing for a few years now wasn't yet another controlled blast or a tame fire, no, this was heavy stuff man. Everywhere that I went it broke out, there was no stopping this crazy blaze! Before I left Lakeland I was sat in a restaurant with a bunch of guys having a meal. Meal times were always interesting and basically looked like me staring into space whilst guys attempted to get my attention whilst all along my food got colder and colder and colder! As I sat there with my head on the table totally trancing out a lady from the UK asked me a question, "So Dave at your next Sloshfest will you be doing any outreach mobilisation?" A legitimate question I suppose, I mean if you are starting to see stuff then why wouldn't you want to take it onto the streets? Suddenly I heard myself saying out loud, "Naaaaaaar I've done mobilisation, I'm going for immobilisation, It's time for the church to get out of the way!" Instantly as I said it there was some sort of crazy chain reaction that happened in the room, it seemed that there was so much weight on those words that a physical wave suddenly rolled through that restaurant which hit guys on the left and the right. Chairs started rattling, tables started rattling and complete strangers all over the room just started laughing uncontrollably. Immobilisation! What I was experiencing was new, I had no handle on it, I had no idea how to walk in it or channel it, it was crazy and was just breaking out wherever we went!

As I came back to the UK I was fully aware that the weight of glory on me was stronger than ever. In a few weeks time we would be hosting our second Sloshfest in Llanelli, Wales to be attended by about 500 guys from all over the world. People were starting to wake up, guys were beginning to find

10 - YouTube - "Deceptive Wine from Lakeland" https://www.youtube.com/watch?v=Af82HUus3UA

themselves overtaken by this wine and were starting to lose all sense of inhibition and religious pride. We just knew that this Sloshie was gonna pop. Our first Sloshie a year before was raw and blunt, guys had no idea what they were signing up for and we had no idea how many would be even remotely interested in attending. This one had a totally different feel to it, there was a feeling of momentum and excitement, word had spread globally without any need of a future social media avenue. One guy who was speaking arrived a day early with a word that Wales was about to see a 'New Welsh Revival!' He was super excited and it all added to a very present *now* reality! By this time I had been intoxicated for months, there was a realm which I seemed to live in which didn't seem to dissipate, neither did it's presence seem dependent upon my religious efforts to maintain it!

Hundreds showed up, this thing was drunk. Many came in fancy dress, it was blatantly obvious that this was all about the party, all about a celebration! Pretty much everyone seated on the front row of the meetings was dressed as monks! Speaker after speaker attempted to communicate their revelation of the Gospel as wave after wave of glory rolled through the hall. One night as Benjamin Dunn led us in worship hundreds of people went into some sort of crazy corporate trance situation. It was strange to watch and even stranger to be a part of. It looked so similar to a swirling mass of starlings as they all flocked together and began to almost synchronise in mid-air. This hypnotic realm of reality involving about 300 guys lasted for hours. In the middle of the tangled mess guys found themselves being pulled into visions of heavenly bliss and some received crazy spontaneous healings. The glory was so strong that night that the speaker came forward and shared with me that this whole realm was something they had never experienced before so they felt unable to speak in that atmosphere! Can you imagine that? I mean these were the sweetest, drunkest and craziest guys that we could find and even they did not have a clue of how to react

to such an ecstatic reality. The noise all week was unbearable. At one point person after person came forward and confessed with the microphone that they were 'evil free!' It was so exhilarating to hear guys confess one after the other that they were totally free from any bondage at all! How glorious is that!

The highlight of the week had to be the appearance of a guy who said that he had been drawn to the event! He stood up on the first day and shared how that in the worship he had been spontaneously healed of deafness in his one ear AND that his veins which were collapsed due to years of heroin use had popped back into life! This guy was funny, what was even more funny was him standing there in front of 500 guys saying, "Anyone here can cut me, I challenge anyone to cut me, you'll see that I will bleed for the first time in an age, my veins are back!"

It all got crazier as that night a guy walked into the hall in the middle of one of Winnie Banov's preaches, apparently the man was a taxi driver who came to collect the strange guy and take him home. All of a sudden in front of 500 people the strange guy who was now hammered drunk walked up to the taxi driver, jumps on his back and starts riding him around the front of the church all the while slapping his backside as the whole congregation cheered and clapped him on wildly! Winnie then shouted out, "Get the taxi driver God! You monks on the front row go and get him!" Suddenly the poor cab driver has one guy riding him around and 5 monks jumping all over him! Eventually the poor cab driver fell to the floor with all of us piled on top of him then he suddenly leapt up whilst looking at his hand and runs out of the hall as we all laughed like little kids! Little did we all know that he had actually broken his thumb as he fell! Neither did we know until a few weeks later as I read the local newspaper and recognised the picture attached to a story written there, that the crazy guy was actually on the run from an open

prison and was a well known criminal who specialised in fraud and deception! I love the randomness of an intoxicated life!

A year later we hosted our third Sloshie this time in Sheffield, England! By now *'Operation Immobilisation'* was in full swing, all over the world people were going out and purchasing wheel chairs to aid them in their intoxication. I bought 4 and by the end of the campaign was pretty good at gauging a good one from a bad one! I actually had a great deal on one wheelchair which I bought for just £60, I was so chuffed with the deal that I had, the chair was like new and still had the protective plastic on the arms! I purchased one of the chairs on the way to a meeting one day from a real sweet girl who had bought a better one for herself! The girl was so sweet and I ended up buying her old wheelchair for £20 then laying hands on her for her healing ensuring that her new chair was also available for purchase! Now I do understand that the idea in most meetings is that the anointing rolls in and the minister gets to pray for the sick and those who are infirm get to wheel out their empty wheelchair! Not in our meetings! In our meeting guys would be so hammered that they would be rolled into the meeting in the wheelchair and would remain there all day! It was crazy, guys were calling me from all over the UK with super excited voices hurriedly explaining to me the type, colour and wheel size of their brand spanking new wheelchairs! We even had a pit stop team at some meetings who were on hand to help with any breakdowns or issues with tyre pressure!

This Sloshfest would be called *'Operation Immobilisation!'* On the big screen behind the stage was a huge picture of a wheel chair with the words *'Operation Immobilisation'* placed around it! The kids loved it, they just got into those chairs and had chariot ride races all around the hall as guys attempted to preach! I needed continual care at that Sloshfest so I was given a delegated nurse who cared for my every need as I sat in my

wheel chair with a catheter dangling between my legs! This thing was stupid, why Dave why do it? Well because it was drunk, because it was fun and because we were all DONE with the boredom of the religious bullshit which held so many in bondage! At the time I suppose we attempted to prophetically justify some of our actions, looking back I now realise that we were just breaking away from manipulation and control and probably didn't know how to handle our freedom in any other way than doing stupid things together! That Sloshie was fun. One night the glory hit so heavy that we all held some sort of 'counsel' on the stage as we deliberated how to move the meeting forwards!

As we rolled into 2010 we decided to hold another Sloshfest in Barry, Wales. By now we had taken this crazy intoxication all over the world and although there was always a new stream of guys who were 'getting it' I had the sense that things were beginning to get stale. Man I know that the party never ends, that the Good News is ever present and that it is always just that, *Good News*, I just realised that in some respects this thing had now massively popped, it now needed teachers and pastors who could raise up the banks and allow this thing to gain momentum via teaching and revelation. Looking back I now realise that in some respects I'm just a fore-runner and that I had done my job in helping to break something new through within the church. I also began to realise that now was the time to look for other areas of life to influence, I mean the world is a big place right? The Barry Sloshie was fun, guys came again from all over the world and the small Dolphin Club where the event was held was rammed to capacity. Again guys came dressed as all sorts, pirates, monks, nuns, a guy came dressed as Abraham Lincoln and we also had an *Electric Man* pay us a visit! *Electrics* was another level! He showed up wearing black tights, a black top, a

Jesters hat, a pair of zebra print boots, whilst all along sporting a long wire of flashing Christmas tree lights! I liked him, he seemed the sort of person you could trust, so I immediately gave him the microphone and asked him to share!

By now we were starting to get a lot of media attention. The church in the UK held no interest for the media, it was all the same old same old traditional rhetoric. Our arrival on the scene was different, we were obviously very unusual and made room for a new type of story. A media team showed up from England who were filming a documentary of Crowder's ministry called '*The YouTube Prophet*!' They brought with them a couple of girls from a University who were studying theology yet considered themselves atheists and a couple of young guys who considered themselves drunken hedonists wanting to see if they would experience anything at the event. Within minutes of the boys being present a whole bunch of Sloshie attendees gathered around them and blasted them with the new wine. They got hammered drunk and later confessed to feeling *something* impact them!

A few weeks before the event I'd been approached by The Sun Newspaper. The Sun is the largest daily newspaper in the UK and in the top ten daily newspapers in the world. This was a pretty big deal and would prove to have massive ramifications for me personally. So many people feared that it would be a bad move allowing the paper access, as some disliked their style of reporting, but hey by this point of my journey I had nothing to lose, I had no reputation as such and just wanted to have fun! I opened the door for the paper to come through and drunkenly encouraged the attendees on the first day by singing the song, "The Sun has got it's hat on hip-hip-hip hooray, The Sun has got it's hat on and it's coming out to play!" There was no need to get intense, no going back down that road, I had learned that

great things happen as you just enjoy life, that seriousness was a problem and that sobriety was a real issue!

The reporter from the paper was a real sweet Irish guy by the name of David Lowe, I instantly knew that I could trust him and felt totally at ease as he walked around the congregation chatting with the revellers! I knew that this was going to work out well for us, we had not come this far to have everything destroyed and who cared about that anyway! Sloshfest blew up and a few days later right in the middle of The Sun newspaper was aired the story 'Holy ravers who get high on God!'[11] It was the sweetest write up and depiction of the event that we could have possibly asked for! Even someone who would have been on board with us at the event, a great linguist, author and orator like John Crowder could not have penciled in a greater depiction of the event. I was named as the 'Event Organiser,' John Crowder the 'YouTube Prophet' and Benjamin Dunn the 'Crowd Pleaser!' Hilarious stuff, we were just having fun but these guys gave us titles! I soon realised that most people would have been willing to pay a small fortune to have that type of free advertising! Two full pages going out to millions of people, C'mon! I just sat back and wondered what would come from it all!

11 - The Sun Newspaper (London: News Group Newspapers Ltd. HQ), 2009.

# Chapter Eleven

## BIG BROTHER OPENS IT'S DOORS TO THE WHACK

*"I can see a door opening for you into the media, I don't think anything like this has been done before! It's not something that will be shared on Christian television, neither is it something on YouTube, this will be different!"*

It was January 2010, here I was in Rome, Italy sat with my dear friends Jason and Heather and suddenly Heather speaks these words over me. A few weeks before, back in Wales, I had dreamt something strange which had got my attention. I love the dream realm! I have learned over the years to pay attention to my dreams and to allow myself to be sensitive to this super highway of prophetic information which opens up in the night watches. Donna and I had gone through a horrific 7 year boundary dispute with a neighbour and our dreams proved to have an integral part to play in knowing what direction to take. One night in a dream I saw a lady show up at the back of my home, I saw her face, how she was dressed and overheard a conversation that she was having. The following day as I walked

down my drive there was that exact lady, dressed just how I had seen her the night before having the exact conversation! I knew exactly what to say and do! Stuff like that always happens to me in dreams, I love that realm and have received much prophetic insight via this avenue of heavenly communication.

A few weeks before Heather spoke these words I received a dream where I saw a very wealthy businessman rock up to a TV Studio to do an interview regarding business and his life. As the man was half way through talking about his business suddenly a wave of glory hit the interview and instantly the man was covered in a heavy deposit of tangible gold dust! It was very obvious to all watching that this was amazingly supernatural! The man then turned to the camera and said, "This is the glory of God manifesting in this place, right now in your homes receive the presence of God through your TV screens!" As I woke from that dream I realised that God was going to open a door into that whole media realm and that somehow His glory would be felt by guys in their homes!

Benjamin Dunn had asked me to go to Rome with him, he was there with John Crowder and a whole bunch of interns. He knew that I needed cheering up, it was pretty obvious that it was the end of a season and the future, although glorious, was somewhat uncertain. I had loved the Sloshfest season of my life, I knew that really it was just an extension of my own personal bliss being offered to a wider audience but I knew that this realm had now been opened to others and that it was time to move on. I was aware that there was a great big world full of amazing people out there and knew that in reality they also needed to experience this presence! Breaking away from convention is never easy but is always essential if we are to evolve and grow. All too often people fail to walk in the fullness of all available to them because they allow themselves to remain trapped within the walls of convention. Sadly this is most clearly portrayed

within the realm of Christian ministry where ministry usually looks like an event where a bloke wearing an expensive suit stands to share a plausible message whereby he strengthens the conditioned thinking in the masses. Few ministers actually break from this convention, few minister to those who are desperately needy and broken, and so the cycle repeats itself! I was beginning to realise that there was a great big world outside of the 4 walls of Christendom and that few were actually taking the time to go there!

The time in Rome was wild, every day on the trains and buses the glory would break out, one day an entire bus load of guys got hit as a few of us just goofed around in the glory. The day after Heather spoke those words I called home to chat with Donna, the first thing that she said to me was, "The casting director of the Reality TV program Big Brother[12] has been on the phone, she wants to talk with you about the possibility of you being part of this years program!" I instantly knew that this was the fulfilment of the word spoken by Heather and that this would be the next step for me. As I sat on the plane making my way back to the UK I suddenly found myself expanded in the Spirit, I became aware that I was sat on a throne above the media mountain and I knew that I would begin to have something of an influence via that arena. On my return the casting director called me and asked me some questions, "So is this stuff true do you get drunk in the Spirit? I've watched 3 days of your YouTube videos is this stuff real? Listen 100,000 queue for up to 9 hours for a 2 minute audition to be on the program, what if I allow you to skip that entire process and you just come to London and meet with the producers of the show? We are really interested in speaking with you!"

Big Brother had made a huge splash 10 years previously in the UK. It was such an unusual concept which seemed to make for

12 - Big Brother (UK) (Amsterdam: Endemol, Apollo Global Management), 2010.

uncomfortable yet addictive viewing. It started as some social, media experiment which eventually blew up and went global. Stick a bunch of guys in a house, deprive them of all interaction with the outside world, starve them of certain basic items and privileges, make sure you put in a crazy mixture of characters and personalities, light the magic touch paper and stand back ready for the explosion! Each episode is watched by millions each day in the UK and what was going to cause a huge draw this year was going to be the fact that this would be the last year that Channel 4[13] in the UK would host the program and the last year that the legend personality Davina McCall would be presenting the show. Big money was to be thrown at this series, it was the end of an era and Channel 4 were promising that they were going to be pulling out all the stops!

A car load of us drove to London to meet with the series producers. I wore my monks robe and showed up hammered drunk at Wembley arena. As soon as we arrived I was greeted by a crazy sign, there was a beautiful black Rolls Royce parked right outside the arena sporting a number plate which read 'David!' As I walked into the hall I was asked to complete a short application form which was taken off me and whisked away. Everyone I met that day seemed to know me, it was strange, it was as if they had all been told that I was arriving and that I would be on the show? I'm not sure if that was the case, it could just have been me sensing a lot of destiny on the whole thing! As I went in to meet with the staff who were interviewing me they seemed interested in asking me a few more questions based upon what I had written on my application form - "I see that you have written down for the question '3 interesting facts about me,' that firstly, I spend days laid on my sofa hammered drunk on God?" I just looked up and said, "Yes that's correct!" They moved on, "Secondly you say that you travel through time and space?" I answered again, "Yes I realise that I'm a son of

13 - Channel 4 (Channel 4 Television Corporation).

God and all things are possible to me!" They then asked me a question regarding the third point on my application form, "You then go on to say that the third interesting fact about you is that the furthest place you have ever visited is the sun? Is that true?" I just laughed and confirmed my answer! They seemed to all like me! They thanked me for my time and said that I would be going through to the next phase of the audition process to be held in a few weeks time.

It's amazing how uncomfortable people become as you begin to walk out into new areas. So many who are not doing anything themselves will always attempt to instruct you on the impossibility of what you are about to venture into. Few had faith that anything good could come from me finding my way onto the Big Brother stage. If I had listened to many around me I would have shrunk back immediately! If it wasn't for the fact that I continually felt in that enlarged state, perched right above that media mountain with a grace of super confidence at work inside me then I would have crumbled to nothing. "What about your family? What about your ministry? What about your marriage? What if it all goes totally wrong?" Man I had heard all of this stuff a million times before, if I'd have listened to those voices then I would never have left my secular employment, never have stepped out into ministry, never have put on that first Sloshfest, never have attended Rodney's conference in London! Few liked the idea. My mother who was a massive Big Brother fan herself loved the idea, she was totally on board and started having visions of meeting Davina and George Lamb!

*A word of encouragement. Years back I would occasionally go and visit this awesome old guy called Eric. Eric was an amazing chap and always found time to encourage me in a time when I was still pooping green and found myself spiritually wet behind the ears! I would regularly go and visit Eric and his wife Maureen and would always love and appreciate my time with them. Eric was*

*of a different generation but back in his day he saw a great move of the Spirit. I suppose the dynamics of faith and transformation remain the same even if the circumstances and time-frames may shift a little! Eric would take me into a little caravan on his drive and together we would listen to Ern Baxter teachings and compare notes. One day as we sat there Eric said something to me which I will always remember. As he looked at me that day this old and wise sage just said, "just because you have a vision from heaven don't expect guys to jump over themselves to come and support you, YOU will need to start running with the vision, then when it's a success others will come and jump on board!" I knew what he was saying. It's amazing how few guys will help you when all you have is a vision? Many will offer advice, few who carry real faith, fewer still will jump on board. Whatever the vision that's burning in your heart today do not search too hard for an endorsement and a helping hand from others, just go do whatever is in your heart and once it's a success others will soon gather around you.*

The guys from Big Brother never told me that I would be going into the house, even on the live launch night there were 81 of us in the audience and only 14 of us were certain to go through those doors 'apparently' by random selection! I already knew that I was going in - there were too many incidents, too many moments and too much glory on me to suggest otherwise. The Big Brother guys continually told me not to mention to anyone that I had a chance of being part of the show. If anything leaked to the media then your chances of being part of the program were dashed. I didn't care, everywhere I went I told guys, as did John Crowder who once announced it to a bunch of Bethel students as he preached to them! Donna and I would be out having a meal and I would start talking with the waiters, "Hey you watch Big Brother? I'll be on that this year!" They would then want a picture taken with me whilst all along Donna would be growling at me from across the table and kicking me right in the shins! Once a guy came from the north of England to buy a

rifle off me. As he was leaving I said to him, "Hey you watch Big Brother?" He just looked at me and said, "I don't but the Mrs is a huge fan!" I continued, "Well I'll be on it this year do you want a picture with me?" He did and on the live launch night as I walked into the house wearing my monk's robe the guy says to his wife, "I know that guy," to which she replied, "How? He's from Wales!" He then whipped out his phone and showed her the picture we had taken together!

Over a 6 month period before I entered the Big Brother house I knew that I would be going in. The faith and desire that I felt combined with the reality that I was continually in an expanded condition sat in the heavens was proof enough! A few days before I was due to leave for London for the live launch night for the program I invited 50 guys to my home for a chat and a celebration. That night I shared with them all (most for the first time,) that I was going away for a while to appear on Big Brother and I asked them to do all that they could to support Donna and the kids in my absence. Many looked at me with strange expressions on their faces, some needed a 'chat' with me when others had left! It was funny but I was encouraged that Donna and I had so many great friends in our lives! It had always felt real to me, from the moment that Donna told me that I had received the phone call the future reality was strong on the inside of me. Now I was about to leave my family for almost 80 days to appear on one of the UK's most controversial and strongly opinionated programs. This was it, no looking back now!

For 2 days 81 of us were in a lock down situation. Hopefuls from all over the world were present all desiring that opportunity to appear on the last ever Big Brother to be aired on Channel 4. I really felt for some of the guys there, they were so looking at this opportunity to be the one big break which would change everything for them. Some of those present had auditioned year

after year, some had been short listed several times yet never made the show. One girl in particular from Ireland was absolutely buzzing, she was convinced that this was her year and that this would change everything for her and her young children, it never happened for her. I was placed in a group with about 6 others. In that group was a real cool guy who had appeared on another reality program years before and had been scouted and short-listed for this year. I loved him, he was an amazing character with a great big heart of love! He also never made it. I was later told that he had so struggled with the disappointment of not making the program that he threw himself under a train! So sad, he was such a sweet guy! The lock down was fun but intense. I was used to being around big characters and even bigger egos but it soon became obvious to me that these guys were REAL characters. After 10 years of airing the Big Brother program the casting team had learned exactly who to choose and what dynamics were essential in making a great series! These guys knew exactly who and what they were looking for! All of the 81 hopefuls carried huge personalities and it was obvious that life in the house wasn't going to be easy for whoever made it that year!

81 waited patiently to have their name called live on television but only 14 would initially enter the Big Brother house. I was chilled right out knowing that I would soon be called forward whilst others bit their nails in eager anticipation! Some went forward to loud cheers and others to a barrage of boos and jeers! Soon I heard the words, "Big Brother chooses you Dave Vaughan!" My face was shown on the big screen as was my video introduction and up the stairs I went to a mixture of boos and cheers and I entered the Big Brother house. Although I knew that I would be entering the house and although I had seen and lived that moment a million times in my mind nothing could prepare me for the strangeness of that moment! I was walking into the Big Brother house barefoot, wearing a monk's robe,

rigged with a microphone, with over 50 cameras at the ready and a whole bunch of weird strangers waiting to meet me, with whom I would be eating, sleeping and showering with for 77 days solid! Do you know how strange that is? The moment the doors shut I felt as if I was in a crucible of pressure! Gone were my family, gone were my friends, gone were my privileges, whatever I said and however I came across was about to be scrutinised live on TV and broadcast all over the media for the whole world to see!

It was a strange environment to say the least, squirrelled away with a whole bunch of individuals who I didn't know, all wondering who would sleep where, who would eat what and ultimately who would crack first. I had no sleep at all for the first 3 days! It was high intensity craziness and in the back of my mind I knew that the cameras never slept! It probably took me about 3 weeks to settle down; it was tough in there, I was used to being locked up in my room for hours every day 'huffing' on the baby Jesus and here I was being massively exposed to ordinary humans!

Each week we voted two guys up for eviction and each of the first 3 weeks I was up for eviction! I'm not surprised, they must have all thought that I was a total weirdo! Twice I won a task to swap my eviction, once I was voted to stay in by the public! After 3 weeks I suddenly felt at home and the love of God started to hit the house! One day one of my best friends in the house walked into the kitchen, he was a real 'toff,' a private school boy who walked around as if he had a silver spoon hanging around his neck and a plum stuck in his mouth! I loved him and we got on great. As he walked into the kitchen he said to me, "Brother there are two types of fathers. There are fathers who usurp themselves as fathers because they are older than others, and there are fathers who are voted as fathers by those around them because of who they are and what they carry. You are of

the second type brother and we honour you as a father in the house!" Man that touched me and showed that the love of God had started to manifest in the house and that guys were starting to respect who I was and what I carried.

Each year the Big Brother house would get a title from the public and media based upon whatever it was that was predominantly manifesting within it's walls, our year was given the title of the *House of Love*! Davina would ask guys evicted why the house was so loving and tactile saying that it was by far the most tactile house they had ever seen, people would answer that it was because I was in there and that as long as I was there the house would remain a *House of Love*! All the while this was all going out to the British public via the media. The Big Brother producers soon realised that the house was way too loving and caring! They thought that their viewing figures depended upon controversy and scandal so they purposed to send in a guy who would stir stuff up. It changed nothing and the love remained and the viewing figures were better than they had been in years!

It wasn't an easy experience. 77 days of sleep deprivation, food rationing, social bullying and intense isolation from the freedom to do whatever you liked was not easy. All the while I was left wondering how my family were and what was going on in the outside world. Big Brother would constantly mess with your head - remember this is something of a social and psychological experiment and we were the guinea pigs. We would watch as one individual would be singled out to have pressure put on them. Over the period of a week or so they would be prodded, prodded and prodded some more until they eventually popped! It wasn't pleasant for us but hey this was a TV program and having people viewing was essential. I had my own battles whilst I was in there. I'm a family man, I love my wife and kids so it wasn't easy to be without them. Big

Brother used these factors as a way of getting into my mind and emotions in an incredible way. Once I was given a secret task to get a letter from my kids, it wasn't an easy task and I failed so I was sent into the Diary Room and I had my letter read back to me real fast! This was hard to accept, not nice at all, I loved my kids and so wanted to hear their hearts.

Each week we would be given a 3 day task to complete. Depending on how well we did in the task determined how much money we had for food that week. Some weeks we failed and were given basic rations which were just that *basic*! This particular week we were given a task called 'Ignore the Obvious!' For 3 days all sorts of weird stuff happened in the house and we had to totally ignore it. One day an entire brass band marched through the house, another day a naked guy took a shower whilst we all sat around watching! Some of the guys had relatives and friends show up and they just had to resist talking with them. Then one day a table was set up in the garden with a spread of cream teas placed on it and suddenly Donna and the wife of another contestant walked in! They both sat at the table and for 30 minutes enjoyed tea and cakes together whilst all along I had to resist interacting with Donna or else I could have failed the task! This was 50 days in! I was desperate to hug her! Looking back I now wish that I would just have grabbed her and forgotten all about the task! It was sick!

I would regularly get spiritually drunk in the house. One night I got absolutely hammered on the glory and myself and another contestant sat there and laughed like idiots for a good hour or so. That night I felt the angels coming into the room, I saw them going around to my friend and sensed them standing right next to him. All of a sudden he started laughing and saying, "Monkey man what is going on here? I can feel something pulling on me!" It was fun and it all went out on national television. One day whilst I was there I heard that familiar voice saying, "Go into

the Diary Room and tell them that the floods are coming. There will be flash floods, go and tell them." This was such a big deal for me, I chickened out and have 'sorta' regretted it ever since! The next day I was in the garden with a few of the guys and all of a sudden as we looked up we all saw a huge mass of black clouds rolling towards the house! It was crazy, one guy started freaking out and saying, "Look at those clouds, looks like something from a Hitchcock movie!" Suddenly my eyes were opened and I saw a guy who I know who walks in incredible supernatural stuff, he was sat on a golden throne and was riding the clouds towards the Big Brother house! (I know that sounds crazy and I'm not expecting a single person to believe me but the following day he was with some great friends of mine in Scotland and said to them, "Did you see the floods last night in the Big Brother house? I caused that, ask Dave he saw me!") Suddenly a drop of heavy rain hit the garden, then another, then another! Soon the heavens opened and rain like you have never seen before hit the whole area! Suddenly one of the guys came running into the garden saying, "Guys the house is flooding, come see!" We ran inside only to find several of the rooms had their ceilings split and streams of water were cascading in! The place was totally flooded, the whole house was wrecked! We goofed around in the water until the electrics started flashing and Big Brother told us to get out of the house immediately! We were all evicted from the house and needed that night to sleep in a separate building! Nothing like this had ever happened before or since! The following day headline news was 'Heavens open over the Big Brother House!

To cut a long story short I came out of the Big Brother house as runner up, top man and went further than any family person had ever gone before! I walked out of the house that night to screams and cheers, people outside held up boards which said 'Are you drunk on the monk,' and 'Are you feeling the glory!' It was crazy, the public had somehow adopted me and taken

on board my crazy language! Over 3 million watched that live finale. As I sat there with Davina I had an opportunity to talk for almost 10 minutes about love, family and His presence! Crazily Davina started asking me about 'The glory' and showed a montage of clips called 'Glory Know Your Limits' of me drunk in the house with a guy talking over the top about the affects of the intoxication of heaven! I couldn't believe it, the wine had definitely gone up front and centre! This was crazy, I was just Dave who lay on my sofa and enjoyed His presence and here I was watching the glory getting publicity and honour live on secular television which was being watched by millions of people in their homes! How does that work? I finished my interview and walked back stage with guys screaming out, 'Dave, Dave, Dave!" Man they actually thought that I was a celebrity! All I wanted to do was see my wife!

# Chapter Twelve

## THE FRUIT IS GLORIOUS

Before I went onto the program I heard that voice again and this time it told me that, "The wine is about to speak!" So many looked at the intoxication as foolishness, many still do! People wanted instant results, plausible answers. It's difficult for the church to understand the wisdom of God when it comes in a package which looks reckless and child like! We like to think that we have grown up, we so like to be able to give understanding to people, to have an ability to answer all of the questions. The drunkenness is far from that, it looks immature, it looks silly and begs the question 'how on earth is this profitable?' To lay on a couch for days, weeks and months in an incapacitated state, to be taken far from the place of caring about the very immediate needs manifesting all around the world when at least you could be helping someone, seems immoral and unethical! Yet scripture is full of strange accounts of the wisdom of God manifesting in unreasonable ways to answer the need of the hour. A young lad with a sling defeats a giant, a wild man in the wilderness baptises the rich and wealthy, a rod stretched over a sea causes

the waters to abate, a virgin gives birth to a Saviour in a fricking stable! I always knew that those moments of stillness on the couch were the most profitable of my life. I always knew that the fruit of resting and of realising would somehow bear more fruit than all of my best efforts could muster. Whilst I lay there over those weeks my memory would wander back to Jakarta, back to the office of Pastor Jonathan and I would hear him retell his story one more time, "I had one encounter and my church grew from 197 to 2500 in one year! The harder that I work the less my church grows but the more that I rest and enjoy Him the more that my church grows!"

On the drive home from London we pulled in at a service station. As I walked into the garage to pay for the fuel I noticed that guys were looking at me? That was strange! Whilst I was away in the Big Brother house the new iphone had come out so being the Apple freak that I am I decided to pop into the town and get myself hooked up. As I walked around the shop guys suddenly started walking over to me and asking if they could have a photograph with me or have my autograph. It all seemed a bit strange but I was up for it. Then as I walked out of the shop I suddenly found myself caught up in a scrummage of about 30 guys who were all shouting, "Dave, Dave can I have a picture, please Dave?" It freaked me out! I literally ran back to the car, drove home, ran into the house and just looked at Donna, "Why are you pale? What's wrong?" she asked, "They think that I'm some sort of celebrity, it's crazy!" She just laughed saying, "Babe you were on television for almost 3 months, every day, they're going to think that!" I certainly wasn't expecting that! I knew that some went into the Big Brother house looking for fame but I certainly didn't! My motives were to follow that inner witness, that inner journey deeper into life. Nothing had prepared me for this!

I suddenly found myself thrust into a situation which lasted for months where every day no matter where I went I was literally mobbed! I could visit any town, city or village in the UK and within one hour I would have between 1-200 people stop me for photographs. A few days after I came out of the house John Crowder was holding a *Mystic School* in Cardiff, Wales. Naturally we hooked up and I took him for a coffee. As we walked out of the coffee shop we were suddenly mobbed by a stack of people all wanting photos! John turned into my camera man for about half an hour as the guys waited in line for pictures. As we walked away and queued up to pay for the parking a young girl stood in front of us with her parents, suddenly she turned around, saw me, started screaming and almost passed out!! It was hilarious and left John saying, "A lot of things have changed since the last time I saw you Vaughan!" Every day this would be the series of events!

My great friend Phil Smith couldn't wait to come down and hang out. He drove all the way from Sheffield to Wales just to spend a few days with me. The first night that he arrived I was messaged by a girl who had set up a Twitter account in my honour whilst I was in BB. She and her friends loved me on the show so set up an account and called it 'Glory Girls!' She wasn't a believer but just a regular girl. I took the account over, changed it's name to '@Gloryboybb11' and Phil and I just sat back stunned as in one evening I amassed over 19,000 followers and saw the word 'glory' trend over the whole of Manchester, England! By the end of the second day I had over 32,000 followers! I also set up a Facebook account and within one day I reached my 5,000 person limit without adding a single person myself! The crazy thing was I was only used to hanging out with those I then considered believers or Church guys, but these were all just regular guys who wanted to connect with me! In the first week after coming out of Big Brother I had over 3,000 direct messages and emails from ordinary people asking

how they could know God and connect with this glory! One person messaged saying that her young disabled child would watch the show each night and each time I would come on the screen she would point and get super excited and obviously impacted! It was all pretty overwhelming for me and all a very clear indication that this wine was far from foolish!

I took Phil to Cardiff for the day just to chill out and look around. There was no chance of that! As we walked through the city centre guys just started shouting over the road at me, "Glory! Hey Dave, Glory!" Then another would shout out, "It's all in the Glory isn't it Dave!" Then another guy shouted across the street, "Dave your the new face of Wales, it used to be Tom Jones but now it's you bro'. You've earned our respect and now you're our representative in Wales!" Man how did that happen? As we walked into McDonalds all of heaven broke out! Guys started barging past each other and queuing up to talk with me. There must have been over 100 guys all stood there waiting for a photograph and autograph all saying, "Glory!" It got so crazy in there that the McDonalds staff suddenly found themselves employed as my ushers filtering the people to me in an orderly fashion! As we walked outside and back onto the street the same chaos resumed, then onto the Apple store we saw exactly the same result! Guys just wanted to be with me, to hug me and talk with me. Some called up their mums or dads who were great fans of mine on the show just so that I could talk with them or pray with them. That day we easily hugged over 300 people! None were church people, none religious, these were just ordinary guys who wanted to spend time with me.

It was all a bit crazy! Do you realise how weird it is to be hundreds of miles from home, to walk into a service station toilet and for a complete stranger to open the door for you and say, "There you go Dave?" Now that is crazy! Three times on

the streets of Sydney, Australia I was stopped by random guys asking if they could have their photos with me! Once I was in America at a hotel and I went to the front desk to check in and a girl says, "I know you, you're the monk from Big Brother UK!"

One guy followed me around a sports shop in the States, I clocked him following me and whispering stuff to his partner. He then stopped me and said, "It is you isn't it? You are the monk from BB UK?" It wasn't just that guys were recognising me but also that guys were telling me how impacted they had been as they observed my life on the program. Once I was in a shoe shop in Wales and I saw a guy with his girlfriend acting real strange, they were 'sorta' following me then peering around the boxes of shoes at me whilst saying, "It is him, I know it's him. I gotta talk with him. I'm gonna ask him now!" I could see that they were both too embarrassed to approach me so I just said, "Are you guys ok?" The guy just freaked out and said, "Dave it is you, please can I tell you my story? I used to be a believer, I loved God but my faith got suffocated by the church. I had no interest in spirituality at all, I was just switched off, I was probably hurting after my experience in church. I'm a massive Big Brother fan and started watching your series. I initially hated you! I hated who and what you represented. Over the weeks I started to warm to you though, you seemed ok and I started wanting you to win. Then I realised that every time you came on the television that my heart would start to warm again. One day as I watched you your words suddenly came through the screen and my heart just melted within me! I was instantly transformed and felt born anew! I've now started going back to church and I feel totally different again regarding God. Thank you so much Dave!" Wow, that was some strong wine speaking right there!

I heard so many funny stories from guys regarding my time

in the house. One day a complete stranger called me wanting to tell me what was going on in her little Welsh village! She was so excited as she proceeded to tell me her story, "Dave our village avidly followed you while you were on Big Brother. We loved watching you but it caused a major issue in homes and workplaces in our village. Everyone started to say the word 'glory' A LOT, it wasn't a big deal to start with but then it took over! Suddenly parents found themselves scolding their children for the continual use of the word only then to find themselves, five minutes later, saying it themselves! Work places started to put up 'Glory swear boxes' and every time someone was caught using the word they had to put money in the box for charity! One guy went to the dentist and needed to be put to sleep for an operation. Just as the man was about to go under he suddenly revived and in the middle of the dentist room shouted out 'It's all in the glory!' Dave our village has turned into a Glory Village!"

It was obvious fruit. Big Brother was nothing more than a little key that opened huge doors of opportunity! Guys have given themselves for years, have laboured intensely, have sacrificed so much time away from their loved ones all in the name of ministry and have seen nothing like this! As church leaders the majority of time and focus is usually spent majoring in on a handful of guys who invariably will all be Christians. Few actually make any real inroads into the lives of ordinary, secular HUMANS! For all of our trying to make an impact in many ways the world is still indifferent to the Gospel! Whilst all along the *believers* get fatter between the ears as they belly up to yet another Christian event where they are told the same thing over and over and over! The top Christian celebrities in the world can walk down the streets of the UK and no-one would even know who they are, sadly they've made no impact whatsoever apart from encouraging a tiny minority of church folks. Yet when I came out of Big Brother I worked out that probably 1 in every 6

guys in the UK knew who I was! Can you imagine the doors that this opened up? The invites that I had to attend birthday parties, charity events, celebrity events, all over the UK? Opportunities to hug on people, love on people, endorse and encourage people, lift up the heads of those who felt depressed or troubled! Most of these people would probably never darken a church door or walk into the latest Bethel conference. Leaders still look at me as if I'm nothing, that's OK, I'm not attempting to impress anyone or to win anyone over. They look at the wine as if it's some sort of strange accessory that can be wheeled out in the 'after party' once all the respectable people have gone home to bed! Fuck that stuff man! I'm not ashamed of this intoxication, it's not some weird bolt on or added extra that can be 'used' at an appropriate moment! Hell no, this is life, Mr. Life Himself, REALITY! I always knew that the wine would one day speak, I knew that it would be poured down the necks of amazing, ordinary folks, and here I was watching it break out!

I soon realized that I had been thrown right into the middle of a crazy harvest field of opportunity. Most guys will never see that level of influence because their time is continually spent crying out for the harvest to come in instead of engaging with the harvest. The media loved what was taking place, everywhere that we went a team from some local or national radio station would be present wanting an immediate interview with me. I suddenly found myself in magazines and news articles. 'Sorted' magazine ran a cool double paged article, my story was rammed right in between an interview with Will Smith and an interview with Jackie Chan! I soon started to get invited to charity events and weird celebrity events. They would hire a tuxedo for me and put Donna and I up in a plush 5 star hotel with all expenses covered. At one event I was given a standing ovation as Olly Murs waited on stage to perform. It was all so surreal, I was just

the drunk guy who got my head stuck in a barrel long enough to realise that I was the barrel and that this bliss was eternal! Donna and I would find ourselves at posh dinner parties seated right next to famous actors or musicians being graced with opportunity to just chat and share our hearts. Almost always the conversation would come around to religion or spirituality and we would just dive in and encourage guys on their journey. I would find myself in conversations with CEO's of corporations and with heads of national media organisations in the UK. It was all crazy stuff, totally surreal yet all part of my destiny.

Probably my greatest moment was meeting up with one of my sporting heroes, snooker genius and five time world champion Ronnie O'Sullivan. I had always loved Ronnie. There was just something about him that got my attention. The guy is just so real, wears his heart on his sleeve and plays his sport with a freedom and skill which is second to none. I remember one day watching Sky Sports[14] and seeing in the news that Ronnie had blown up at some event and was in big trouble with the Snooker gods! Ronnie always seemed to be either making news for winning a competition or for doing some strange or naughty act. This seemed to be another of those times as the news rolled across the screen. As I saw it my heart just went out to Ronnie and I realised that I had a real deep desire in me to somehow meet with him and share with him how loved he truly is.

In the September of 2010 John Crowder was holding a *Mystic School* in Sheffield England, I showed up as I always would to hang out with John whilst the school was running. This was the school where a whole bunch of religious nuts stood outside and protested the event. At the time it seemed like a good idea to buy a devil suit from the local town and paint my face as a devil and to stand outside with the protestors holding up my own board which had the words 'Both darkness and religion

14 - *Sky Sports (Sky plc).*

hate John Crowder' written across it! Their faces were a picture as I joined in their protest against John! "How can a devil be on our side?" It was hilarious as I shouted at passers-by not to attend the school because John has done great damage to my camp! Fun, fun, fun! Remember, DO NOT TAKE YOURSELF SO SERIOUSLY!

As the day rolled on in Sheffield we came down in the hotel elevator to go out for dinner and as the elevator doors opened there stood right in front of me with a couple of his friends was Ronnie O'Sullivan! I shouted at him, "I know who you are, you're the 'Rocket' Ronnie O'Sullivan, I love you man, please can I have a picture with you?" Suddenly Ronnie turned around and says, "Man I know who you are, you're the monk from Big Brother! I want my photo with you! You were great on that show, so real, that's why guys loved you and was the reason that you did so well! I want my photo with you!"

It was crazy, I couldn't believe what I was hearing, the great Ronnie O'Sullivan knew who I was? Anyways Ronnie gave me his number and asked me to text him the picture. Later that day I had a text from him asking me if I fancied hanging out with him in the bar that night! Man I was so excited, this was like all of my dreams come true. In one day I got to dress as a devil and protest against John Crowder AND I got to meet my snooker hero Ronnie O'Sullivan. That night I sunk a beer down with Ronnie and spent an hour with him at the hotel talking about snooker, life and the glory! Moments like that are continual reminders that this wine isn't too foolish after all.

There was so much going on that it just seemed right to host a 'Gloryfest' in Wales and to invite the world to come and be part of it! 600 guys showed up from over 30 nations. The party was ense as was the realm of glory that opened over that place. y for the first time heard the Good News of their oneness

with God and many got ecstatically drunk after realising their eternal perfection and laughed for days afterwards! 10 of the Big Brother guys showed up, it was so awesome to see them and for many of my friends to actually meet them in the flesh. It was a crazy event, *Loaded*[15] magazine (a Lad's Mag - soft porn type deal,) sent a reporter and camera man to the event! A few days later right in the middle of their April 2011 edition, squeezed between pictures of ladies' breasts was an amazing 4 page article entitled 'I'm off my tits on God!' It was an awesome article, so well written, surrounded by cool pictures of the event and there it was right in the middle of a bunch of nudity!

Gloryfest blew up! It was a landmark moment for so many on their journey. Off the back of it I felt compelled to write to the Gay magazines introducing myself and apologising for the church's attitude towards their subscribers. I'm believing that one day soon I will get an opportunity to appear in *Attitude*[16] magazine and I will have chance to talk about just how screwed up the church's attitude has been towards the Gay community!

15 - *Loaded Magazine (Borehamwood: Simian Publishing Ltd.), 2011.*

16 - *Attitude Magazine (London: Attitude Media Ltd.)*

# Chapter Thirteen

## STUPID SUPERNATURAL STUFF

Alongside the media attention came an effortless ability to walk in the supernatural. I started to travel a fair bit and wherever I went I saw the craziest manifestations of the Spirit and started to see even weather patterns shift in a crazy way. When you begin to realise that you are one with an eternal source and that you are in no way confined to a physical body things begin to change for you. I mean if you are one with Him, if you are an extension of His reality, if He is in you *as you* and you are in Him and He is everywhere all at the same time, then where are you? Maybe translation in the spirit is nothing more than you realising that you have a desire to be somewhere then realising that you are already there! There is no distance between us, there are no walls that separate our union together. Regularly I will have a desire to connect with someone and I will just allow that desire to manifest to the extent that I feel like I'm actually physically standing right next to them. At times this manifestation has been so strong that guys have text me at that exact moment saying that they can feel me stood right by them!

OK we may not physically feel that we have the capacity to be with someone but in the spirit we are already one and are already connected! As we cultivate that sense of union we can gather with each other as and when we desire!

Something begins to explode as you realise and practice that reality. I have had whole seasons of my life where I was just as aware of walking in the spirit realm as I was walking in the natural realm. Just as you are able to function and move in this earthly realm so you are also able at the same time to function and thrive in the spirit realm. I have never been more aware of this reality than when I visited Australia in 2010 with my great friend Joanne Gravell.

We were visiting Sydney to minister at some gatherings there on the Kings Road! Before we boarded the plane at London Heathrow I walked out of the toilets and was instantly aware that I was in heaven whilst being on earth. As I walked through the airport I was aware that I was fully walking out of a different realm 'into' this earthly realm. It was as if as I walked I carried with me the full bearing of a heavenly authority which carried with it the potential to change everything! It was crazy and as it manifested it came with a tangible and very drunk sense of presence. That whole trip in Sydney was crazily supernatural. I really don't know how much to share in this book but I'm going to push the boat out and I hope you will track with me!

I feel that what Jo and I experienced that week was something of an indication of a potential reality which in the coming years guys will effortlessly walk in! Each day as Jo and I walked around it was so obvious to us that heaven was with us. As I walked down the road I would be fully aware of a full load of glory bearing down upon us, and whoever we came in contact with, which manifested from another realm. As we walked past people it was as if there was something of a crazy reaction that happened in their lives, some would start to chatter and make

funny noises, some would start to laugh and fall around drunk and some would instantly get rooted to the spot and begin to prophecy over us! These people were all complete strangers by the way! As we stood at a counter in a McDonalds one day the girl serving us started to laugh uncontrollably, she then started to prophesy over us with great accuracy, she then fell to the floor and started rolling around and the guys ran from the kitchen and looked at us as if to say, "What is going on with her? What has happened to her?" The girl then got up off the floor and suddenly went all shy like a little child and ran into the kitchen. This stuff happened the whole time we were in Australia.

One night Jo wanted to rest so some guys came to collect me to take me to visit a great church in the area. The whole time I was in the car the glory just increased and increased to the extent that I had to be carried into the meeting. As we walked into the gathering and I attempted to walk to the front, guys just started laughing and getting hammered drunk. My friends sat me on the front row and the leader suddenly took the microphone and asked me to share. Man there was no way that was going to happen! I just looked at the guy next to me and said, "Get me out of here, take me back to the hotel!" I was carried out whilst everyone laughed at me.

That night as I laid on my hotel bed the glory of God came out of the bottom of my feet and filled my hotel room, Jo then called me and said, "Dave the glory has filled my room!" I said, "Yes I know, it came out of the bottom of my feet!" That night I just laid on the bed and vibrated and glowed! The following day Jo knocked my hotel room door and looked at me in horror and said, "Dave you are glowing, turn it down!" I just looked back at her laughing with the words, "I've waited 40 years for this I'm not turning anything down!" This was wild stuff but it was about to get wilder!

We were obviously aware that we were causing a disturbance

in the area! I mean spiritually stuff was shifting. The glory was manifesting heavily in the meetings to the extent that guys were crawling on the floor up the road outside the meeting place and the local witches were showing up for prayer and deliverance! Then on the last night that we were there something absolutely crazy happened which frankly I'm not expecting anyone to believe! It was the final night of our gatherings so the host arranged for a limousine to collect us as a treat! As we walked outside the hotel for our ride we were confronted with a scene where the driver of the limo was repeatedly asking a man to get off the bonnet of the car. The guy was just sat there refusing to move as the driver urged that he stood up. As we walked over to the car another man walked up to me, he looked a little hippyish and wore rough clothes, had dread lock hair and he didn't smell the best! He suddenly addressed me by name and said to me, "Mr. Vaughan it is good to see you! Mr. Vaughan unlike you we are not men under authority. We cruise around Australia looking for people like you Mr. Vaughan so that we can cook you something nice to eat!" The man then started to curse me in some weird language. I was just drunk and laughed at him whilst all along him and his buddy, who had got up from the bonnet of the car, cursed me. Jo just looked at me and hurried me to get in the car!

As the driver took off he was totally freaking out! "Who are those guys? How did he know your name? And how did he appear out of thin air?" That got my attention! "Appear out of thin air? What happened?" The guy looked at us and relayed the events of the night, "Well I was waiting outside to collect you," he said, "then suddenly that man came and sat on the front of my car and refused to leave! Then the second man appeared out of thin air at the exact moment that you walked out of the hotel. He then walked over and called you by name!" As I said I'm not expecting any of you to believe this stuff! If you like I'll write next time about how pleasurable the whale watching was, (well

for me anyway, Jo spent the whole time throwing up over the side of the boat!)

An amazing door of opportunity was opened to us by some dear friends from Fort Wayne, Indiana to build a children's home in the Philippines. We now have our own home full of kids in the nation and there's nothing that we enjoy more than taking a team of guys to the nation where we go party with the kids in the slums and dumps of the area. Every time we go to the nation we see the craziest supernatural stuff and we have great fun together. One year we took a large team and I just sensed that we would see some crazy, crazy stuff. I mean there are times where you just feel that eternal connection so strong, you sense reality all around you and are aware that you are walking straight out of that spirit realm into this natural world. As I arrived at the hotel that first night I just knew for some crazy reason that on this trip the lightnings of God would follow us each day. As I walked into the hotel I just looked at the manager and for some crazy reason I said, "So have the lightnings hit yet?" He just looked at this white boy tourist and said, "Oh I'm sorry sir it's the wrong time of the year, there will be no lightnings!" I just laughed and said, "We will see." An hour later as we walked outside the hotel all across the sky lightnings flashed and thunders rolled!

Each day the lightnings would follow us around! One day we visited our children's home and as we stood there on the ground, without a cloud present in the sky, I looked out and there were the lightnings flashing all through the sky! We then got invited to speak at a church where the meetings were held up on the roof of the building which was all open and exposed. On the way to the meeting as we all sat in the bus I started sharing with the team how it is an amazing revelation that we love God and that we worship Him, but just as amazing was the fact that God

loved us and how He worships and adores us! As we arrived at the building and the meeting started we were suddenly aware of His presence with us, I got up and took the microphone and just felt led to share the thoughts that I communicated on the bus with the team. I just shouted out, "It is an amazing revelation to love God and to worship Him, but just as powerful is the revelation that God loves us and that He worships and adores us!" At that very second, at that exact moment a huge flash of lightning shot across the sky above our heads and the loudest clap of thunder accompanied it!! As you can imagine that meeting suddenly warmed up a little!

I love South Africa, that Biltong is another level of glory! Each time I visit the nation I always see an incredible explosion of the supernatural. My initial draw in going was to connect with the recently transitioned and sweetest guy ever Kobus Van Rensburg. If ever there was a man of faith and reality it was Kobus and I had the pleasure and privilege of meeting with him a few times. Actually in one leaders' conference with over 5,000 leaders present which was being aired all over the world via his TV channel, Kobus called me forward and anointed his water bottle top, squeezing it whilst saying the words, "In Him we live and move and have our being," before he dropped the bottle top into my hand. That was special! Kobus realised the importance of the wine.

As I sat in one of the sessions it quickly became obvious to me that although the teaching was great and the honour in the room incredible that something was wrong. There was no joy in the room, no bliss, it was sad. This is so typical of modern day Charismatic events, oh they will tell you exactly how things must be done, oh they can give you a beautiful theological discourse on so many topics and you may even see an odd healing thrown into the pot, but my question remains 'is it drunk? Where is the

wine?' As I sat in that conference suddenly I heard that familiar voice saying to me, "You have come to this nation to serve it a drink! They need a drink!" Suddenly Kobus took to the stand and said, "Guys there is something missing here, heaven is a party, you all look like you need a drink! Let's sing that song, you know the one band 'Are you ready-ready-ready?' We must have a drink!" Suddenly the band wheeled out Godfrey Birtills song 'Are you ready?' - which he actually wrote after he visited Wales and heard all of the stories of glory breakouts in the nation! That session was instantly transformed as room was made for the wine of heaven! Oh that all ministers would realise the importance of this heavenly intoxication!

The second time I visited the nation I hung out with my good friend Gerhardt Neiuwoudt for over a week and together each day we saw the glory of God break out. It was a wild time together and each day was like one long trance like state. Wherever we went we saw the glory break out. In restaurants we saw such a heavy presence manifest that the waiters would walk past us with their trays and would just start laughing uncontrollably. One lady came to serve us and as she stood there she just totally lost the plot and had to walk away from us, we then heard her in the kitchen laughing and screaming, she was out of control. As we walked into one place I went to take my seat and as I did I just felt the need to get up and to sit around the other side of the table. As we sat there waiting to be served the realm of glory was so strong that a waiter walked out carrying a tray of food that he was about to serve someone, he came near our table, froze like a statue and the food all slid off the tray and smashed on the floor right next to where I would have sat!

One night Gerhardt took me back to my hotel room and the fire of God just hit the place, as we sat there it felt as though a real fire was burning in the room, whilst all along you could hear a strong wind blowing back and forth outside the window. It was

crazy and we needed to take off our jumpers to compensate for the heat!

The whole time I was in the nation we were just under a heavy weight of glory. Creation seemed to continually respond and the weather just shifted as a sign of the craziness. As we drove into Jo'burg for my flight home the weather was incredible, warm, sunny and real nice but I just knew that something was about to happen! I was yet again in that expanded state and I knew there would be a response. I just looked over and said to Gerhardt, "Bro' you watch the shift in weather as we hit Jo'burg, it's gonna be crazy!" We walked into a casino to have a meal and were just chilling out and eating together and above our heads was a TV screen showing footage of a rugby pitch which was being hammered by huge golf ball size hailstones. It looked like there was supposed to be a game being played but it had been cancelled due to the weather. Anyways we just thought it must of been miles away because the weather here in Jo'burg was great! UNTIL we walked outside and right across the sky above our heads was the craziest lightning show you will ever see in your life and huge golf ball size hailstones were raining down all over us! Gerhardt and I just laughed like little kids as we realised that yet again creation responded to the manifestation of our sonship!

A few years ago I got to hang out with the one and only Tim Wright. Tim is the sweetest guy in the world and he heard I would be in the States so he hurriedly set up a few extra days of preaching for me in Pennsylvania! The whole time with Tim was wild, our eyes were continually sealed shut and all Tim did was complain with a drunken slur that he needed his nails done! One day we staggered through a shopping mall together and fell about like little kids to the amusement of all watching especially some young lad who heard us laughing like children

in the rest rooms and was quick to stare at us and say, "What are you guys doing?" Great question son, we is drunk!

One morning I woke up in some basement where Tim had me cooped up and as I staggered around the house I heard myself say over and over again, "Has the storm hit yet? Have I missed the storm?" The guys in the house just looked at me like I'd lost the plot, "What storm Dave?" An hour later we drove down the road to get a coffee, all was fine, the weather was great but then the clouds started to gather right in front of our car! The clouds got thicker and thicker whilst all along the wind picked up and before we knew it lightnings started to flash across the sky and hail in sheets started lashing the car. We laughed together as I said, "I guess this would be the storm then!" As we pulled into the car park of the coffee house we ran inside as the entire staff had their faces pressed against the windows with horror written all over them as they watched the carnage outside! Before we knew it the entire car park was flooded with water. I asked the staff why they were so interested in the storm? Their reply to me was that it hadn't rained for over a month and hadn't thundered in over 3 months!

We saw something similar when we were at Fort Wayne with our great friends Amy and Chad Davis. I was there with Jo Gravell and it was all just one wild drunk time. It was whilst we were on this trip that we went back to our hotel and I opened the door to my room only to find it filled with the glory. That night I had very little sleep as I had encounter after encounter with Martin Luther who, I realised, 500 years before was having the same thoughts as us regarding the need for a radical reformation of the church. The moment that the wheels of our plane touched down in Indiana I felt straight away that I was sat on a throne above the area and that everything that I was doing was coming out of that realm. Let me just say that in no way do our spiritual encounters denote maturity nor do they suggest that some guys

are further up the ladder than others. Hell no, I've made some bad mistakes and in many ways my theology has always been screwed! I just was able to connect with a realm of reality which is available to us all!

Whilst Jo and I were there we experienced some crazy stuff together, we also connected on a cool level with Amy and Chad and it was while we were with them that they offered us the opportunity to build with them in the Philippines. On the last day that we were there Jo was due to fly home and I was needing to be in Alabama for some meetings. Chad offered to come with me to Alabama along with our buddy Nathan Kipfer. As we started off from Fort Wayne I slipped into some sort of trance in the front of the car and put my head down on the dashboard as Chad drove us. Suddenly I felt myself again in that expanded state and I instantly knew that I wouldn't make Alabama and that Jo wouldn't be flying home! As I lifted my head off the dash I said to Chad, "Take us to the airport, Jo will not be flying home and I won't be going to Alabama!" Funnily enough at that exact moment we were right at the turning to the airport and as Chad started to drive towards the terminal a snow storm hit which was so strong that by the time we got there all the flights had been cancelled! We turned back and walked into Chad's home and before we could say a word Jo shouted at me, "This is all your fault!" Jo knew what happened whenever we would travel together!

I've seen all sorts of crazy stuff as I've connected with reality. I'm not saying any of this to boast or to suggest that I'm in a better place than anyone else. I'm just wanting to catalogue my journey and my perceptions, and that's all that these stories are, they are *my perceptions*! My aim via this book is just to encourage the reader that this is your reality, this is your journey, that you are fully human and fully Divine! In the coming days

it will become progressively more difficult for you to ignore your Divinity! The realisation that you are just like your God, that although you are just a drop from the ocean that you are the very ocean itself, that to see you is to see the Divine! We are not being boastful by talking in such terms, this isn't pride, this is reality, a spirituality that transcends any religious order. Jesus didn't come to establish another religion, He came to show and to be an example of a fully human and spiritual life apart from religion! These stories are your portion, whatever you are liking from these stories are what you are desiring in your own spiritual life. I'm hoping that one day I will connect with you all individually and that I get to hear your stories, that I also may grow and be inspired again!

One of the funnest things I ever encounter is what I like to call 'Glory Invasion.' The first time that I saw this manifestation hit it freaked both Phil Smith and myself out! I was hosting some meetings in the Wirral near Liverpool, England and we decided to take guys out to do some evangelistic stuff in the day. I had my monk's robe on and teamed up with Phil to just chat with random guys. We were pretty toasted and it was more than obvious to us that certain guys didn't really want to be seen with us. I understand why! Phil and I walked up to these two men and just started chatting with them, they could see that we were both pretty drunk and they just laughed and mocked us. As we chatted with them they both confessed that they were atheists and that they wanted nothing to do with us.

As we were about to leave the craziest thing which I think I have ever experienced happened! Suddenly it was as if the Spirit of God within me leapt from me and hit the one guy! It was shocking, very tangible and instantly made me think of when Jesus said in scripture that "virtue left Him."[17] We all saw it happen, it was very noticeable! The guy instantly started

17 - Mark 5:30 (King James Bible).

shaking violently and crying in front of his other 'atheist' friend! He then said, "Whatever that is that just hit me I want it please pray for me!" It was an instant turn around and the whole thing left his friend picking his jaw up from the floor! Before I could pray for the guy Phil took my hand and placed it on his own head and said, "I don't know what that was but I want that same stuff to happen in my life please give it to me!" I had nothing to give, I was as shocked as everyone else! I have no key for this manifestation, it's just a weird happening which seems to be linked with the drunkenness and which definitely works!

Godfrey Birtill and I have seen this 'Glory Invasion' manifest a few times when we have been together. Once we were ministering together near Derbyshire in England and there was another conference being held in the same building called *'Has the Church repented enough over it's treatment of Israel that it can now see revival in the UK conference!'* I know, I know!! Where do they get this stuff? In between our drunken sessions Godfrey and I walked outside and a lady from the *other* conference shouted over at Godfrey, "Geoffrey, Geoffrey Birtill it is you isn't it?" I just looked at Godfrey, it was all too much! As you can imagine from the title of the conference she was attending the lady was, let's just say, a little dry! I just looked at her and said, "So how are we doing in the UK? Have we repented enough to see that revival?" Instantly the same manifestation which hit the guy in the Wirral hit that lady, it was as if something jumped off me and hit her so hard that she fell to the ground and started laughing uncontrollably! As she lifted herself off the floor she just looked at us a little sheepishly and walked off in a tizz! Godfrey and I just looked at each other in shock!

In 2010 Godfrey and I were in Charleston in South Carolina together and Godfrey was in a phone shop asking the guy some questions. As I walked into the shop the guy instantly got

hit and started shaking and laughing like a hyena behind the counter. Once again Godfrey and I just looked at each other! I love the effortlessness of this stuff, people wheel out all sorts of programs, formulas and means in an attempt to make something happen. These are usually the same ones who frown upon the intoxication and look at us as if we are stupid when we begin to manifest anything 'unusual!' There's nothing unusual about this glory, the natural mind struggles with it because religion has conditioned it to think that it must work hard to prosper. This is not the case, as a matter of fact the opposite is true! All of our efforts to produce quickly fail, we shift from one project to another and heavily rely upon *our* ability to bring transformation, often the result is burnout and sobriety! There's so much bliss in knowing that of myself I can do nothing! That He said that *He* would build His church. I've seen more fruit as I've rested and enjoyed the life I have been given than all of my striving to produce ever has. As I go to the gym I see the glory break out, as we go out to lunch I see the glory break out, man there's no lack at all in this kingdom! I now realise that ministry is nothing more than me being me wherever I am!

# Chapter Fourteen

## STUPIDLY HILARIOUS STORIES

As I've already suggested in this book, sadly for many the 'fun' has been taken out of 'fundamentalism.' If anything most Christian gatherings are far from fun and they can tend to leave you a little mental! Leaders frown upon anything which is not intensely serious or full of heavy sobriety and in so doing they extract the jam from the middle of your Charismatic doughnut! I realised many years ago that heaven is a *fun* place and that joy is, as C S Lewis suggested, the 'serious business of heaven!' [18]I've noticed over the years that the strangest and weirdest stuff happens as we just enjoy our bliss, Benjamin Dunn would mock Crowder all the time and suggest that a 'Drama Angel' would show up every time John let loose! Drama Angel or not I have noticed that as we just relax and enjoy life that crazy entertainment follows! Invariably guys would always ask the question, "Well what is the point of this? Why do these things happen?" It's hilarious that religion always has to see a *point*

18 - Lewis, C.S. Letters to Malcolm: Chiefly on Prayer (San Diego: Harvest), 1964.

in something in order to just kick back and enjoy the moment! There always has to be a reason for the joy or else it's just relegated as foolishness! Over the years we have found ourselves caught up in all sorts of wild and stupid activity, foolish things, pointless things have broken out all around us! There's been no explanation for these incidents, I haven't looked into them too deeply, they're just moments in life which you look back on years later and as you re-engage that moment you begin to feel that same feeling of drunkenness and hilarity hit you again! It's like the gift which just keeps on giving! I can imagine years after Jesus was crucified the disciples having a 'Jesus reunion meal' and James turns around and looks at Peter and says, "Dude can you remember how we would all be chilled right out around the camp fire with Jesus and then suddenly Judas would start goofing off and lighting up his own farts? Dude you remember Jesus face bro' the first time Judas did that?" I mean come on, often there is no point in stuff other than we are having fun and the craziness is adding to our bliss! Man I love *pointless* religious activity!

There was one church in England where conferences were becoming something of a success and where I would occasionally show up. A friend and I decided to take a day out to travel up to the church one Saturday for a Bobby Conners conference they were hosting. I remember how jacked up we were that day AND just how much food we flew into us. It was crazy, on the way to the meeting we stopped off and had a mega English breakfast with all the trimmings and the obligatory heavy latte. Then after the first session we hooked up with a guy who told us that he was staying at a local hotel who were serving an 'eat all you can roast buffet!' It sounded great so we thought we would give it a try! The food was amazing, all sorts of meats, roast potatoes, gravy, stuffing, oh and of course the obligatory heavy latte!

We rocked up to the next session with our bellies bursting with food and our hearts filled with joy! That session I asked Bobby Conners for his watch, I didn't get it! Before the last session we decide that we should probably eat yet again even though it was not that necessary! I knew of a real nice curry house in the area so off we went, I ordered the usual, Onion Bhajee starter, Chicken Vindaloo, Keema Fried Rice and a big fat Garlic and Keema Naan bread! All was washed down with an ice cold pint of ale and we managed to stop off at a coffee shop on the way back to the venue for the obligatory heavy latte!

By now I felt ready to pop, I had no room left for the wafer thin mint! Walking back to the conference my belly resembled that of something sported by a 70's wrestler in the UK. I was FULL! It was one of those moments where you are actually afraid that you may have done yourself a mischief! It felt as if the food and liquids were pushing themselves back up and were resting somewhere near my adam's apple!

By this point in my journey lots of guys were aware of who I was, so often I would be approached by others asking if I would pray for them, this night was no different and immediately as I walked into the back of the building a lady approached me. She told me that there was a team of pastors from India in the meeting and that she had told them what was breaking out in Wales and had suggested that maybe I would pray for them. I was more than willing although I was feeling awfully full and nastily uncomfortable!

As the Indian pastors walked over to me I started to pray over them whilst for some crazy reason shouting the word 'LOOOOOOOSE!' All seemed great, one after another they fell over in fits of laughter! As I prayed with the last guy and he fell backwards somehow he grabbed my hand and I ended up on all fours on top of him with my head somewhere near his crotch area! Suddenly I released the impartation along with

the 'LOOOOOOOOSE!' Oh it got loosed alright, instantly from within the very deep of my being a dark brown, lumpy, frothy, coffee coloured concoction projectiled itself out of my mouth and straight into the crotch of the dear Indian pastor! I looked up and about 30 guys were stood around us 'sorta' laughing, 'sorta' cringing and 'sorta' questioning what I was about to do next! I mean what would you do? The guy is laid there in his best suit, his crotch is soaked with lumpy, coffee froth and I'm kneeling over him feeling like a total idiot! I decided that the honourable thing to do was to attempt to spoon the mixture from his trousers as best I could and then, mmmm not sure what to do then, with it all over my hands but hey one step at a time! The pastor seemed to know that I was uncomfortable with this, whilst obviously being very uncomfortable with it himself! He just looked up and smiled and said, "It's ok you can leave it!" We both walked into the toilet to get cleaned up!

As I sat down in the congregation it was obvious that I smelt pretty bad! The fact that every man and his dog were offering me mints bore testimony to that fact! Suddenly the host of the meeting says from the platform, "I am so pleased to announce that tonight we have with us some very special guests. All the way from India we have a team of amazing pastors!" I knew what was about to happen! I sunk into my seat and prayed to Mary for grace! "Will all of our Indian friends please come up on the stage and greet the people!" My worst nightmare! There he goes, wet crotch and all, up on the stage to greet 1,500 people, several of whom saw me vomit into his crotch and who were all looking at me as if I had committed some hideous crime! Poor fella!!!

This is just one incident, there are many! After the 'Closer to the Flame' conference it felt so right to hurriedly host another gathering. We did and by now people from all over the world were interested in what was taking place so we attracted quite

an international congregation. We had all sorts show up, it was a right carnival of life and was full of characters, you could say that it was a *mixed bag*! One woman in-particular caught my attention as she danced at the front of the hall whilst all the time her eyes were rolling around in her head and she made some weird noises. I 'sorta' felt that we needed to keep an eye on her so one lady was assigned to watch out for her! We were never any good at hosting these things, I was always too hammered and made mistake after mistake. This thing was raw and at times must have been very hard to watch!

I decided to call up a guy from Germany asking him to come and share his heart with us. He was pretty toasted and was a genuinely lovely guy although he sometimes talked about stuff which was for many 'a bit out there!' I think it was Rick Joyner who once said that, "Some intercessors are so far out there that God doesn't even know what they are doing!" This may have been one of those cases!

As the guy started to share everything seemed OK, the congregation started to laugh and all was good, until he started to say, "If you cannot handle the sheep anointing how will you ever handle the goat anointing? And if you cannot handle the goat anointing then how will you ever handle the mule anointing!" As I looked over the people all of whom were attempting to be generous but all of whom sat there with blank expressions as the tumbleweed rolled by, I just thought to myself, "I hate my life, earth swallow me up, there is no God!" It got worse, the guy then carries on! Oh he was not finished, that was just the warm up! "You may not be able to receive this," thanks for warning us, I suppose that should be seen as a positive, "but earlier today one of our team had a vision, she saw the Holy Spirit with His trousers down and He was running around the meeting!" At that point I just knew that I had to step in, I laid hands on the guy and

as he fell I caught the microphone and quickly said to the people that it was time to move on!

Little did I know but at that exact moment at the back of the hall the crazy woman who I told someone to monitor was caught with her skirt pulled up and her pants down about to take a pee in the corner of the room! I know, you couldn't make this stuff up! The lady who was shadowing her stopped her and asked what the hell she was doing! Her answer was, "I felt the Lord telling me that I needed to pee in the 4 corners of the hall to mark my territory! Then that man from Germany confirmed the word by saying that he saw the Holy Spirit with His trousers down running around the meeting!" Cuckoo, Cuckoo! Shit happens I suppose!

Our meetings would get out of control, I like that, the only problem is the wilder that things get the more chance there is for collateral damage! Twice in meetings I have had my ribs broke, twice it was when things got wild at the altar! Once the whole of the front of the church turned into some sort of wild WWF slam down. As I ran across the altar and attempted to do a belly flop on top of our friend Jim Drown he brought his knee up and instantly popped all my ribs. The second time I was in the Wirral near Liverpool and was just laid out at the altar wearing my monk's robe and the pastor of the church decided that it would be a great idea to run over and jump straight on top of me. I felt my chest crush on impact and that time my ribs took 6 months to heal. As our meetings got out of control strange happenings would take place.

One weird manifestation which started to naturally happen in our gatherings was what I termed 'Pirate Circles!' These circles of people would naturally form as the glory would manifest and the love for each other would increase and start to flow. Guys would just start to hug each other and then large groups would

congregate and find themselves in huge circles dancing and singing together. It was all fun stuff, very drunk, but I suppose may have raised a few eyebrows for a first time visitor!

One of those visitors was my friend and all round crazy mystic Jason Westerfield who later confessed to initially not having a clue what was going on in our meetings! Jason was initially *concerned* and curious with what he saw manifesting with us. I understand, I mean it was nuts, you had monks, nuns, pirates, an electric man, a guy walking around with a Cheerio box stuck on his head, a Scull and Crossbones flag being raised and lowered at the back of the hall whilst all along the pirate circles flowed! Jason sat there in a trance as the *worship* popped and as he sat there he was suddenly aware of Jesus walking around the congregation with His chest puffed out looking as if He was checking out the weirdness of the party! Well at least there was a party for Him to check out I suppose? I guess most congregations wouldn't even have a party for Jesus to examine? Suddenly Jesus asked Jason a question, "Jason what do you think about this?" Jason being the man of wisdom that he is answered, "I don't know Lord, what do you think?" Shrewd!!! Jesus just looked at Jason as He walked around the pirate circles, chaos and utter foolishness and answered with 3 words, "I like it!" This alleviated Jason's concerns and after he shared the experience with us also confirmed to us that this wine is far from foolishness!

Bob Jones was a real precious guy. Bob was a prophet who walked in much love and who transitioned on Valentine's Day 2014. I loved Bob, loved his anointing and the way that he so effortlessly shared the supernatural with others. I always wanted to meet Bob and a few years back I had that opportunity. For about a year I would show up at gatherings and person after person prophesied over me that I was about to meet with Bob

Jones. Man I was stoked and got even more excited when Jeff Jansen called me and asked if I wanted to go over to America to hang with him at a conference that he was hosting alongside Bob Jones! I soon booked a ticket and bought an expensive Welsh sword to present to Bob because apparently that's the thing to do when you meet the prophet, you take him yet another sword for him to stack with all his other swords in his sword room!

The first night we were there I got to present Bob with the sword in front of about 800 guys. It was an amazing privilege for me but better still was to come. The following morning as I walked into the hotel restaurant for breakfast sat right there was Bob and his wife Bonnie! There he was, man what a moment! Bonnie then asked me if I would like to join her and Bob for breakfast! Man this was heaven, I was meeting my hero. I just sat there and watched Bob as he ate and ate and ate and ate and every now and again would ask Bonnie a question, "Where's them sausages? They said them sausages would be ready by now, where's them sausages?" I didn't want to break in on Bobs ecstatic breakfast but I just had to chat with him, maybe he would give me a word? Maybe he would impart that eagle anointing? "So Bob have you seen anything for Wales?" He quickly answered with a grunt, "Nope!" I then fired another at him, "So Bob you know a mutual friend of ours called Gary, he sends his love," again he barked his answer at me, "Nope!" I continued, "Yes you know him Bob I saw a picture of you and him at your house!" This time he sort of yelled at me, "I said Nope!" I had waited for this moment for years, I had dreamt about it, had visions about it, it was now happening and it looked nothing like I anticipated! What can you do! After a few days I did actually connect with Bob, oil flowed out of his hands and he rubbed them on me for good luck! What an amazing character who will be missed by many.

Our 'ministry' cruises were always a fun thing to do, we saw the world, enjoyed the sun and we had nothing to arrange as all of the administration was adequately taken care of by our sweet friends Danny and Shana Orser. It was via these cruises that Donna and I got the opportunity to develop new friendships and got time alone as a couple. Part of the itinerary for our first cruise was that whilst the boat docked in Belize, as a team we would visit the nation and do some outreach amongst the locals. Everything was set up and Donna and I left the boat with a rucksack full of sweets for the local kids in the area. We found ourselves placed in a team alongside a few other guys and had a local missionary guy with us who led the way. Suddenly as we walked up the road we saw a bus full of kids coming towards us which stopped and parked up. We instantly seized the opportunity to jump on the bus and to start launching sweets at the poor kids on board. I was the first on the bus and I just started throwing handfuls of candy all over the place, I was quickly joined by Donna and a few others and before we knew it there were arms and hands through the bus windows and buckets of sweets were launched out.

With all of our zeal and drunken fervour at one point it all got a big chaotic as handfuls of candy were launched at the kids only for it to smack them up the side of their heads and land on the floor all around them! It didn't take me long to discern that something was wrong, I mean here we were in a third world country and we are throwing sweets out at kids and yet they aren't catching a single one? I mean kids are kids all over the world right? They all like candy right? Yet I observed that as we threw out the candy the kids seemed apathetic towards our generosity and seemed to rather allow the candy to bounce off their heads and chests rather than catch a single one! It was a weird situation and as we left the bus we were all left to scratch our heads in wonderment at what had just taken place! Suddenly our missionary friend appeared from up the street and excitedly

asked us, "So hey did you just have fun giving out candy to all those deaf and blind kids?" Our hearts sank! Here we were attempting to be a blessing to the kids of the nation only to realise that we were actually doing more harm than good. As we joked about it afterwards we soon realised that this was pretty much what we had been doing with the church for a few years! Yes we had spent years throwing out gospel candy to blind and deaf parishioners who refused to catch it, unwrap it and enjoy it!

A drunk man will do things that a sober man would never consider! One day as Donna and I walked down a busy city centre I found myself being strangely drawn into a tattoo shop. I mean I was hammered drunk and whenever I was in that predicament anything could happen! This tattoo shop was the sort of place that doubled up as a piercing station and I suddenly found myself stood at the counter of the shop asking someone how much it would cost for me to have my nipple pierced! Donna just looked at me and said nothing! Within minutes I found myself sat in a chair with a clamp on me teat and a woman pushing a bar into my left nipple! I was bandaged up, paid and as Donna and I left the shop and walked down the road she stared at me as her tongue was loosed and said, "So do you mind telling me what that was all about?" I then heard the words, "When you were young you dressed yourself and went wherever you wanted too, but when you are older another will dress you and take you where you wouldn't choose to go!" I just looked at Donna and told her that I didn't have a clue what was happening! (Ironically a little while after that I was pulled into Big Brother, a way that I certainly didn't choose!) In all fairness I attempted to make out that it was all some prophetic act but in reality I was just drunk! Soon after that I walked into my bathroom and looked in the mirror and saw a white, milky

substance coming from the nipple! All of my prophetic paranoia bells rang as I thought, "Man it really is a sign, I'm beginning to lactate!" I then realised that actually my teat was a bit sore and as I took the nipple ring out puss squirted all over the bathroom mirror! Some stuff is prophetic, some stuff pathetic, or should that be pussthetic!

In 2010 I was holding a tour in the States with Godfrey Birtill and John Scotland! It was all blowing up and we were seeing some cool stuff! The last place on the tour was a trip to Morning Star. John Scotland had a connection there and had hired a room for a couple of days of meetings. We showed up after a long drive both drunk and tired. We actually arrived at Morning Star on the very night where each year they all have a special ball. Everyone was there Bob Jones, Rick Joyner, Todd Bentley and all were dressed in very nice Tuxedos and ball gowns! As we arrived we realised that the only way we could get to our rooms was by wheeling our suitcases right past the function, I mean right past! I had with me a crazy purple striped suitcase which was stinking dirty and falling apart. I didn't want to do it, so embarrassing having to roll this thing right past all these guys dressed in their best threads! Suddenly the punk in Godfrey started to manifest, the crazy, the forerunner, "Come on Dave lad, they're only people, let's get in there lad!" Godfrey grabbed my suitcase, sticks his northern head down and marched past the dignitaries manifesting the attitude of a very young Johnny Rotten! Man we were all so proud of Godfrey UNTIL we noticed that stuck to his backside by a lump of chewing gum was an old carrier bag which must have rustled away as Godfrey marched past everyone! It was hilarious! So proud of old Godders!

A couple of times we have had incidents with animals. Some great friends of ours race and break in horses in the UK. We

regularly visit them and occasionally we will go and look at their ponies. One day I laid hands on one and the thing started to zonk out under the glory! Another weekend we decided to host an event at a retreat centre and we invited Andre and Mary-Ann Rabe in to share with us. Whilst we were there our friends told us that in a few hours time they had a horse running and that the race would be shown on television. We all decided to head off to the television room and 30 of us squeezed in and waited for the race to begin. There was a lot of whack in that room and a lot of anticipation as the race got under way. The horse was doing so well and we were all getting pretty excited so we just started to cheer and urge the horse on. I then told everyone to stretch their hands out to the horse and to start praying for it! "Get it Lord, hit the horse, get it God!" As we all shouted at the screen suddenly and for no reason at all the horse just fell over! It was crazy, there were no fences near and there was no reason other than the fact that the horse just got zapped by the glory for the poor animal to fall. I looked up and all eyes in the room were on me as if it was all my fault. I quickly apologised for making such a poor decision!

One day Phil Smith decided to come down from Leeds and hang out with myself and Jason Westerfield. We spent the night in Jason's hotel room and all I can say is that the glory was intense! As we left early in the morning it was pretty obvious that we were hammered drunk and were walking in a totally different realm. At 6am we walked into my kitchen and my two black dogs started to go crazy! They bounced up to us and just went berserk! Suddenly as Phil and I both looked at the dogs right in front of our eyes the dogs turned an electric blue colour! It was nuts, it was as if they were somehow responding to the realm which had opened to us and whatever was happening with them was causing them to change colour! At one point they

both turned back to black except the very tip of the one dogs tail which continued to remain bright blue! It was hilarious. Then as I attempted to go to bed the dogs were so keen to get to me that they actually ripped the door frame apart as they did all that they could to follow me up stairs! Creation responds again! So glad that Phil was with me this time just to confirm that I was not going insane!

Whenever John Crowder, Benjamin Dunn and I get together something is pretty much guaranteed to happen. Benjamin was asked to do some meetings in Seoul, Korea and he wanted John and I to tag along and have some fun. It was a crazy time and the meetings popped. In the evenings the pastor would take us along to a real nice Spa in the area. This place was nice, full of saunas and steam rooms all heated at differing temperatures. Guys would go there and just relax with friends and family and it had a cool atmosphere about it! The only issue was that it was a *naked spa*! Guys on one side, girls on another and a wall in between! Although the 3 of us had known each other for a couple of years by this point we had never actually got naked together! It was 'sorta' awkward to say the least! I guess it's just a male pride thing as most men would admit to comparing and taking notes in some areas! Pastor Kim spoke very, very little English so as he stood there fully unfurled he motioned erratically with his hands that we were to be *fully naked*, not even swimming trunks allowed! It was soon pretty obvious where we all registered on the 'pecker order,' and just who it was who may have been left languishing on the 'peanut gallery!' Suddenly the slightly animated Pastor Kim takes a-hold of my soft Peter and starts pulling on it as if he was starting up a garden lawnmower! To say that I was slightly put out by this may be an under statement! Then as if by magic his very broken English vanishes and with the eloquence of an Oxford don he starts to

scream out, "Impartation, impartation, impartation!" John and Benjamin just rolled as the guy shook my dong like a bell ringer would swing on a rope at an Anglican church come Sunday morning! This was all well and good but I did not expect to show up at his church the following day as Pastor Kim took the microphone to watch him making crazy hand gestures and laughing as he retells the entire story to the congregation who just looked over at us laughing! 'Impartation, Impartation!' Hey I probably shouldn't have shared that story, it may shed a bad light upon parts of my anatomy, but hey I'm way past caring and you may never know the impartation may have worked!! All you guys reading this who need a 'body elongation miracle' right now just lay hands on that part and I will declare over you, "Impartation, impartation, impartation!"

So many stories to share, maybe I'll share more in another book depending on how this one goes. I'll finish with this story from our last trip in India! John, Benjamin and I took a team of guys into Hyderabad and visited the leper colonies and slums in the region. It was a blast and as always it was crazy fun! John and I then flew into Mumbai where we visited with John's children's home for a day before we both headed off for home. We arrived into Mumbai late in the night and were taken to the sketchiest of little villages and the dirtiest of little hotels! All I remember is that the bed in the room had a weird stain on the mattress and as we turned it over we saw that the bed had a pool of vomit on it which hadn't been cleaned up and which had soaked right through the mattress! It was late at night but we were pretty jacked and there was no chance of sleeping on that mattress, so we ventured out into the night and into a village which resembled something from 'Apocalypse Now!' The pot holed roads were stacked high on both sides with smouldering rubbish piles which had packs of dirty mongrels sifting through

STUPIDLY HILARIOUS STORIES

them all fighting over the scraps they found. Fires burned all over the roads and gangs of hyped up teenagers drove past us on mopeds shouting and laughing.

Only once before have I been on a mission trip where I felt uncomfortable and knew that I could be in trouble, that was years earlier when John and I were in Yemen in the middle of a war zone as gangs of youths walked around us carrying AK47's and huge knives! I remember sitting on my bed that night realising that I may not be going home to see my family!

This had a similar feel to it, this wasn't downtown Mumbai at all, this was different and made us both feel somewhat uneasy! Little did we know that this was the eve of the Ganesh festival, a massive deal in the Hindu calendar and a time where families and towns do all that they can to create beautiful shrines in honour of this deity. John and I flagged down a rickshaw driver who 'sorta' spoke a little English and we told him to take us on a tour. It was 3am, the roads were dark, yet seemed full of activity. We just trusted this guy to take us around a strange town and show us the sights, all the while hoping that he wouldn't take us somewhere where we would be kidnapped or robbed! Every now and again the driver would stop, turn off his rickshaw and say, "Come, come, come!" Then he would lead John and I down a little path or alley and there in front of us would be a blue tarpaulin which doubled as a door to someone's hurriedly prepared, yet beautifully manufactured Ganesh temple! As we would walk in the delight upon the faces of the families inside who for the first time had huge white Westerners visiting their humble construction was incredible! Every family loved us and every family urged us to go back the following year! We visited many of these temples that night, each was different and each time we realised that humanity was full of love and that we are all one even if our worship leads us in different directions!

It had been a great night, it was almost 6am and we were ready

to go back to our hotel, until suddenly we heard what sounded like a huge band playing music which seemed to be parading down the street behind us! As we looked back we realised that a procession of about 100 guys was coming towards us, all were dancing and banging cymbals together and the rolling ark of Ganesh was trundling along behind them! Before we knew what was happening we were suddenly caught up in this wild procession! There we were dancing and hugging all of these jacked up worshippers who were so ecstatically happy that they had such unusual visitors with them on this special night! John and I just went with it, we weren't Ganesh worshippers but we were lovers of humanity and we did realise that maybe the only way that these guys would ever connect with our reality was if we were there with them showing them unconditional love!

Before we knew it the whole thing got out of control, suddenly we had guys grab our hands and start spinning us around wildly in circles! Then I started jumping on the backs of the worshippers and started riding them wildly around the streets! I had no clue how they were going to react but they just loved it and responded with love and care! Before we knew it we were the ones who had the cymbals in our hands and were the ones being encouraged to lead the party! Lead it we did, for about an hour! All the while hugging and kissing these precious worshippers! As the procession ended we realised that we had somehow managed to connect with humanity in an amazing way, right in the midst of their worship and feast! They loved us and with hearts filled with love they looked at John and I and thanked us sincerely for being willing to visit them on their special day. They begged us to return, maybe one day we will!

The whole thing was drunk and right outside the box! If you think about it for too long it seems so wrong, YET it was so right! Religious fundamentalists talk so much about seeing people of another religion transformed and *converted*, yet these would

be the same ones who would frown upon us connecting with others in such a way! I thank John Crowder for being willing to unwaveringly and without question go with that moment. Few would have! Sadly most Christians still live out of their natural mind and are unable to flow with the Spirit, my hope in sharing these stories is that this mentality will break, that guys will realise that the wine is far from foolishness and that it is actually the very wisdom of God. I also hope that through my vulnerability and honesty that guys will stop taking themselves too seriously! Yes you can be a great spiritual giant who sees incredible supernatural stuff but please do us all a favour and just chillax a little!

# Chapter Fifteen

## WE ARE ALL ON A JOURNEY

In some ways I see this book as a parting gift to a Christianity and a religious system which I have loved, served and which has helped me massively in my journey. Much of the language and terminology which I have offered in this book in some ways I no longer identify with and struggle to still endorse. I wanted to use the publishing of this book to draw a line under my past and to honestly share my perceptions of my journey up until this point. Over the years I have encountered so much and I knew that I carried many stories which I believed could help, encourage and humour many. I have no regrets, I can now see that every phase of my evolution has been an essential one. Everything has worked in my favour, even the chapter where I talk about those dark times which I encountered as I came under the domination of a crazed religious system has ultimately helped me to become everything that I am today.

I struggle these days to see truth as an absolute or a doctrine. For me Truth is a reality, its a reality which can be beautifully

embodied by anyone, even those who we are quick to write me off because they are on a different page. I believe that we may not all be on the same page but that we are all on the same journey. All of humanity is waking up to reality, many are beginning to *realise*, some are from within religious structures which we have been quick to write off. At the same time many within Christian circles who feel that they have some sort of ownership on God are struggling to move forward, they find themselves trapped behind thick walls of extreme dogma and heavy blankets of conditioned thinking. There is little room within those spheres for difference and very few are actually being encouraged to think for themselves and to question the status quo. I'm living in a season where I have many questions and I'm beginning to realise that God isn't threatened by my curiosity.

I was massively impacted by something which I heard Martin Scott say as he stood up to preach once. He started his sermon by saying, "What I'm about to share with you today I didn't believe 6 months ago and I may not believe it in 6 months time, but for where I'm at right now this is all I've got!" I love that! Few are honest enough to admit that they have an ever evolving perspective of God and of scripture. The church system is fuelled by an illusion that *you need*, and it propagates a dependency on something outside of yourself. You are taught that you need to attend, you need to listen to this teaching, you need to buy this book, you need to register for this conference, you need to tithe, you need to gather! The whole religious system stands upon a foundation that you must adhere to survive and that without subscribing to the next great *whatever* that you will miss out! I guess that I'm just ready to move on from that stuff. As a matter of fact I feel that I have already moved on from that stuff!

I'm beginning to realise that there is a possibility for spirituality

apart from a need to be attached to a religious system. I'm beginning to see that all religions are man's attempt to give a framework and structure to a perception which is special for them, but that ultimately there is a God and a reality which transcends it all. For years I felt a heart felt connection with the Christian religion, in some respects I still do! Much of the terminology which I have used in this book is because of the mental container which was formed within me due to my connection with a religious system. You may say that Christianity is not a religion and I understand why you would say that! I mean if you have been massively impacted by an element of teaching or via a revelation released with a certain Christian focus then why wouldn't you eat the entire feast offered? Yet you cannot get away from the fact that Christianity is very broad with many denominations, many branches of thought, multiple translations of scripture, thousands of differing opinions on so many so called *truths*! I once said to someone who was avidly contesting that Christianity wasn't a religion that I could prove to her that it was, I just suggested locking 100 'believers' in a room, leave them in there for a few days and just watch how heated the debate would become! Who would be right? I believe that we are now living in a moment of time where we will see the crutches of religious structure which we once relied upon and leaned upon for spiritual endorsement start to crumble all around us.

I'm not suggesting that I have some strain of *new thought* or that I'm *enlightened* in some special way. I'm not offering some path which has been unknown for generations but is now being opened to a select few. Hell no, in many ways I have way more questions than answers right now, yet I look at some of my present uncertainty as a beautiful indication of a green light of freedom to begin to journey and to move forward. As humanity we have to begin to make room for difference!

# Tales from the Couch

## MEMOIRS OF A DRUNK MONK

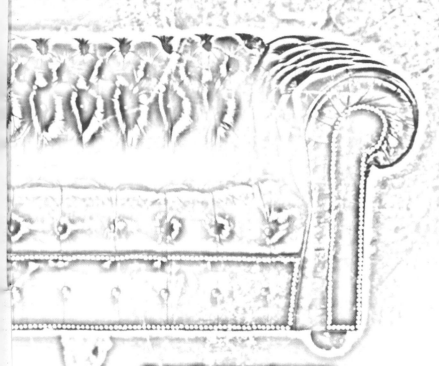

# DAVE VAUGHAN
## FOREWORD BY BENJAMIN DUNN